"Congress shall make
no law...abridging the
freedom of speech, or of
the press."

First Amendment to the U.S. Constitution

The basic foundation of our democracy is the First
Amendment guarantee of freedom of expression.
The Opposing Viewpoints Series is dedicated to the
concept of this basic freedom and the idea that it is
more important to practice it than to enshrine it.

Contents

Why Consider Opposing Viewpoints?   9

Introduction   12

Chapter 1: Is the American Lifestyle Sustainable?

Chapter Preface   17

1. America's Reliance on Oil Is Unsustainable   19
   Emma Davy

2. America Can Safely Rely on Growing Oil Reserves 25
   Robert L. Bradley Jr.

3. The American Lifestyle Is Destroying the
   Environment   30
   Derrick Z. Jackson

4. America Does Not Face an Environmental Crisis   34
   Stephen Moore

5. Nuclear Power Can Be Used to Meet America's
   Energy Requirements   41
   Tom Solon

6. Nuclear Power Is Expensive and Unsafe   44
   Dan Becker

Periodical Bibliography   48

**Chapter 2: What Role Will Technology Play in
America's Future?**

Chapter Preface   50

1. Genetically Engineered Foods Will Benefit
   Americans   52
   Linda Bren

2. Genetically Engineered Foods Will Harm
   Americans   61
   Jeffrey M. Smith

3. Hydrogen Will Be the Answer to America's
   Energy Problems   67
   Julian Gresser and James A. Cusumano

4. Hydrogen Will Not Be the Answer to America's
   Energy Problems   78
   Michael Behar

5. Gas-Electric Hybrid Automobiles Will Help
   Reduce U.S. Oil Use   88
   Lester R. Brown

6. Nanotechnology Will Benefit Americans in the
   Twenty-First Century   93
   Morgan O'Rourke

7. Space Exploration Will Play an Important Role in
   America's Future   100
   National Aeronautics and Space Administration

Periodical Bibliography   107

**Chapter 3: How Can Life for Americans Be
Improved?**
Chapter Preface   109

1. America Should Move Toward a Socialized
   Health Care System   111
   Paul Krugman

2. America's Health Care System Should Not Be
   Socialized   115
   Jane Orient

3. Strict Limits Should Be Imposed on Immigration   120
   Steven A. Camarota

4. Strict Limits Should Not Be Imposed on
   Immigration   128
   Jacob G. Hornberger

5. America's Education System Must Be Improved   135
   Koret Task Force on K–12 Education

6. America's Education System Has Improved   142
   James B. Hunt Jr.

7. Diverting Money into Private Accounts Would
   Strengthen Social Security   147
   George W. Bush

8. Diverting Money into Private Accounts Would
   Weaken Social Security   153
   Douglas Holbrook

Periodical Bibliography   159

**Chapter 4: What Type of Foreign Policy Should
the United States Pursue?**

Chapter Preface   161

1. Spreading Democracy Overseas Will Enhance
   U.S. Security   163
   George W. Bush

2. Spreading Democracy Overseas Will Not Enhance
   U.S. Security   170
   Gerard Alexander

3. U.S. Foreign Policy Should Be Based on
   Preemption and Unilateralism   178
   Victor Davis Hanson

4. U.S. Foreign Policy Should Not Be Based on
   Preemption and Unilateralism   184
   Craig Eisendrath

5. The United States Should Improve Its Relationship
   with Europe   193
   Jessica T. Matthews

6. U.S. Actions Cannot Reduce European Anti-
   Americanism   201
   Russell A. Berman

Periodical Bibliography   208

For Further Discussion   209
Organizations to Contact   211
Bibliography of Books   216
Index   219

Why Consider Opposing Viewpoints?

"The only way in which a human being can make some approach to knowing the whole of a subject is by hearing what can be said about it by persons of every variety of opinion and studying all modes in which it can be looked at by every character of mind. No wise man ever acquired his wisdom in any mode but this."

John Stuart Mill

In our media-intensive culture it is not difficult to find differing opinions. Thousands of newspapers and magazines and dozens of radio and television talk shows resound with differing points of view. The difficulty lies in deciding which opinion to agree with and which "experts" seem the most credible. The more inundated we become with differing opinions and claims, the more essential it is to hone critical reading and thinking skills to evaluate these ideas. Opposing Viewpoints books address this problem directly by presenting stimulating debates that can be used to enhance and teach these skills. The varied opinions contained in each book examine many different aspects of a single issue. While examining these conveniently edited opposing views, readers can develop critical thinking skills such as the ability to compare and contrast authors' credibility, facts, argumentation styles, use of persuasive techniques, and other stylistic tools. In short, the Opposing Viewpoints Series is an ideal way to attain the higher-level thinking and reading skills so essential in a culture of diverse and contradictory opinions.

In addition to providing a tool for critical thinking, Opposing Viewpoints books challenge readers to question their own strongly held opinions and assumptions. Most people form their opinions on the basis of upbringing, peer pressure, and personal, cultural, or professional bias. By reading carefully balanced opposing views, readers must directly confront new ideas as well as the opinions of those with whom they disagree. This is not to simplistically argue that everyone who reads opposing views will—or should—change his or her opinion. Instead, the series enhances readers' understanding of their own views by encouraging confrontation with opposing ideas. Careful examination of others' views can lead to the readers' understanding of the logical inconsistencies in their own opinions, perspective on why they hold an opinion, and the consideration of the possibility that their opinion requires further evaluation.

Evaluating Other Opinions

To ensure that this type of examination occurs, Opposing Viewpoints books present all types of opinions. Prominent spokespeople on different sides of each issue as well as well-known professionals from many disciplines challenge the reader. An additional goal of the series is to provide a forum for other, less known, or even unpopular viewpoints. The opinion of an ordinary person who has had to make the decision to cut off life support from a terminally ill relative, for example, may be just as valuable and provide just as much insight as a medical ethicist's professional opinion. The editors have two additional purposes in including these less known views. One, the editors encourage readers to respect others' opinions—even when not enhanced by professional credibility. It is only by reading or listening to and objectively evaluating others' ideas that one can determine whether they are worthy of consideration. Two, the inclusion of such viewpoints encourages the important critical thinking skill of objectively evaluating an author's credentials and bias. This evaluation will illuminate an author's reasons for taking a particular stance on an issue and will aid in readers' evaluation of the author's ideas.

It is our hope that these books will give readers a deeper understanding of the issues debated and an appreciation of the complexity of even seemingly simple issues when good and honest people disagree. This awareness is particularly important in a democratic society such as ours in which people enter into public debate to determine the common good. Those with whom one disagrees should not be regarded as enemies but rather as people whose views deserve careful examination and may shed light on one's own.

Thomas Jefferson once said that "difference of opinion leads to inquiry, and inquiry to truth." Jefferson, a broadly educated man, argued that "if a nation expects to be ignorant and free . . . it expects what never was and never will be." As individuals and as a nation, it is imperative that we consider the opinions of others and examine them with skill and discernment. The Opposing Viewpoints Series is intended to help readers achieve this goal.

David L. Bender and Bruno Leone,
Founders

Introduction

"From the moment speech began, human culture has evolved. Indeed, society cannot continue without communication. Landmarks in communication have transformed civilization significantly."

—V. V. Raman, *"Milestones of Twentieth-Century Science and Technology,"* World & I, *May 2000*

As America moves forward in the twenty-first century, many forces are changing the way Americans live. The availability of natural resources, technological innovations, government policies, and America's interactions with other countries are all influencing life in the United States. New communications technology is a particularly striking example of a force for social change. Cell phones and wireless and digital technology are rapidly and dramatically altering the way Americans communicate. However, many experts believe that the Internet will have the greatest impact on society.

In 2004 the Pew Internet and American Life Project surveyed Americans about their Internet use and found that this technology is holding an increasingly central position in many lives. Eighty-eight percent of Americans said the Internet plays a role in their daily routines. The activities they identified as most significant are communicating with family and friends, and finding information. Sixty-four percent of Internet users said their daily routines and activities would be affected if they could no longer use the Internet. As the Internet becomes central to communication and the spread of information in the United States, there is disagreement over how it will affect society. Some see a bright future where the Internet facilitates democracy and enhances social interaction. Others fear that the Internet will simply advance the status quo and will cause social isolation. This conflict mirrors many of the conflicts over societal change in the twenty-first century, with some people embracing change unequivocally and others questioning whether change is inherently beneficial.

Many people believe that the increasing prevalence of Internet technology will be greatly beneficial to America. They argue that it will enhance democracy because it encourages the free exchange of ideas. Author Howard Rheingold explains why the exchange of ideas is important to democracy. "Democracy is not just about voting for our leaders," he says. "Democracy is about citizens who have the information and freedom of communication they need to govern themselves." In Rheingold's opinion, the Internet is a way of disseminating that information. He argues,

> The problem with the public sphere during the past sixty years of broadcast communications has been that a small number of people have wielded communication technology to mold the public opinion of entire populations. The means of creating and distributing the kind of media content that could influence public opinion—magazines, newspapers, radio and television stations—were too expensive for any but a few. Just as books were once too expensive for any but a few. The PC and the Internet changed that.

Rheingold and others believe that the Internet destroys broadcast monopolies because it allows any individual with a computer and an Internet connection to create and distribute information to the public. Journalist Bruce Sterling elaborates on this free exchange of ideas that the Internet facilitates. "Why do people want to be 'on the Internet?'" he asks. "One of the main reasons is simple freedom. The Internet is a rare example of a true, modern, functional anarchy. There is no 'Internet Inc.' There are no official censors, no bosses, no board of directors, no stockholders. In principle, any node can speak as a peer to any other node, as long as it obeys the rules . . . which are strictly technical, not social or political."

However, critics contend that while in theory the Internet may aid the free exchange of ideas and limit the influence of individual broadcast companies, in reality this is frequently not the case. Researcher Joanne Jacobs points out that "participation in this kind of [Internet-facilitated] democracy must be confined to those people who have access to the funds for purchase of computer equipment, and literacy in the technology to take an active role in information exchange." In addition, some studies show that among those people who are using the Internet to access information, the majority are not being exposed to a diverse variety of viewpoints but are still receiving most of their information from a few broadcast companies. Clyde Wayne Crews Jr., director of technology studies at the Cato Institute, explains:

> Despite customization, people migrate to popular cyber-realms. Portals duplicate one another, expanding our common frame of reference. Diverse news sites . . . rely on news-gathering organizations like AP [Associated Press] and Reuters that assure common experiences despite filtering. While it's true that more than 600 Web sites get over a million monthly visitors, the top 14 account for 60 percent of online time.

In addition to facilitating the spread of ideas, the Internet has also become a popular medium for social interaction. This has led to concern that choosing correspondence via a computer over face-to-face interaction will create social isolation. As career and personal coach Mary Jo Marchionni explains, "[The Internet] allows us to be isolated from activities that once required participating in the world, such as grocery shopping." Numerous studies support the view that the Internet leads to social isolation. According to a report by the Stanford Institute for the Quantitative Study of Society, "The more time people spend using the Internet . . . the more they lose contact with their social environment." The study found that "this effect is noticeable even with just 2–5 Internet hours/week, and it rises substantially for those spending more that 10 hours/week, of whom up to 15 percent report a decrease in social activities." Johann Christoph Arnold, a social critic and author, agrees that increased Internet use leads to decreased social interaction. "The time we spend on the computer cuts down on the time we could devote to a spouse, child or coworker who might be sitting right next to us," Arnold maintains.

Proponents of the Internet disagree with critics, however, arguing that the Internet is actually being used in a way that enhances social interaction. According to researchers John A. Bargh and Katelyn Y.A. McKenna, fears that the Internet creates social isolation are unfounded. They point to history as proof. According to them, "Each new technological advance in communications of the past 200 years—the telegraph, telephone, radio, motion pictures, television, and most recently the Internet—was met with concerns about its potential to weaken community ties." But instead of weakening these ties, experience shows that each new form of communication has actually strengthened them, say Bargh and McKenna. "If anything, the Internet . . . has facilitated communication and thus close ties between family and friends," they maintain, "especially those too far away to visit in person on a regular basis. The Internet can be fertile territory for the formation of new relationships as well." According to Tom R. Tyler, professor of psychology at New York University, Americans actually use the Internet as a tool for strengthening and increasing their social interactions. "The Internet provides people with a technology that allows them to engage in activities that they have already had ways to engage in but provides them with some added efficiencies and opportunities to tailor their interactions to better meet their needs," he asserts. "The research . . . suggests that people generally incorporate the Internet into their social 'toolkit' and use it in conjunction with face-to-face, telephone, and mail communication to deal with personal and interpersonal issues in their lives."

Despite disagreement, experts agree on one point: As America moves into the twenty-first century the Internet will certainly become more central to the way society communicates. This anthology examines other factors that will likely shape America's future. The authors of *Opposing Viewpoints: America in the Twenty-First Century* present conflicting answers to the following questions: Is the American Lifestyle Sustainable? What Role Will Technology Play in America's Future? How Can Life for Americans Be Improved? and What Type of Foreign Policy Should the United States Pursue? Communications technology and many other advances will contribute to shaping America's future in the years ahead.

CHAPTER 1

Is the American Lifestyle Sustainable?

Chapter Preface

Pure air consists of 21 percent oxygen, 78 percent nitrogen, and traces of other gases such as argon, carbon dioxide, and water vapor. Every day, each person in America breathes between five thousand and fifteen thousand liters of air. The air Americans breathe, however, is not pure. It contains hundreds of chemical and biological pollutants emitted into the atmosphere by human activities. Included in the substances that Americans breathe into their lungs are ozone, sulphur dioxide, carbon monoxide, and toxic metals. These substances can cause various health problems, ranging from mild irritation to the respiratory tract to lung cancer and cardiovascular disease. As the U.S. population continues to expand, motor vehicles, power plants, and industries burn increasing amounts of fossil fuels, contributing to the buildup of these chemicals in the air. Beginning in 1970 with the passage of the Clean Air Act, the U.S. government has enacted numerous regulations to reduce air pollution in America. Despite these actions, though, there remains serious debate over whether or not air pollution continues to threaten Americans' health.

Joel Schwartz, former staff scientist for the Coalition for Clean Air, believes that the United States is "winning the war on air pollution." He dismisses fears about harmful air quality, maintaining that such concerns are based on a misreading of statistics, which actually show that air quality is improving. Governmental policy expert Gregg Easterbrook also argues that the United States has made significant progress in reducing pollution. "Arguably the greatest postwar achievement of the U.S. government and of the policy community is ever-cleaner air and water, accomplished amidst population and economic growth," he contends. Journalist Jonathan Rauch echoes this point of view. "Emissions of all the major air pollutants are way down since 1970," he claims, "even though the population has grown by almost a third and vehicle-miles and gross domestic product have more than doubled."

Many environmentalists contend that regardless of any reductions in pollution levels, America's air is still extremely polluted and is a serious threat to human health. According to the American Lung Association, in 2003 more than half of Americans were breathing air that was harmful to their health. Air pollution expert Arthur L. Williams concludes that "in spite of the considerable improvements that we have achieved, clean, healthful air nationwide still eludes us." Bernie Fischlowitz of the Earth Policy Institute compares the impact of air pollution to other major causes of death. "In the United States, traffic fatalities total just over 40,000 per year," he argues, "while air pollution claims 70,000 lives annually. U.S. air pollution deaths are equal to deaths from breast cancer and prostate cancer combined."

Air quality is part of a much larger debate over whether the American lifestyle is sustainable. As the U.S. population continues to grow and use more and more resources, there is increasing disagreement over whether these resources will run out. The authors in the following chapter explore various facets of this contentious topic.

"World oil production will peak in about 2030. . . . After that, output will decline."

America's Reliance on Oil Is Unsustainable

Emma Davy

The world's supply of oil is limited, maintains Emma Davy in the following viewpoint, and the United States is likely to run out of this fuel some time in the twenty-first century. In addition, asserts Davy, as oil supplies are used up, the remaining oil will become more difficult and costly to extract. Given that the United States uses 25 percent of the world's oil supply despite the fact that it has only 4 percent of the earth's population, America will feel oil shortages most acutely, Davy claims. She suggests that America develop renewable energy sources as an alternative to rapidly depleting oil supplies. Davy is a contributing writer for *Current Science*, a newsmagazine that offers articles for youth on science, health, and technology.

As you read, consider the following questions:

1. According to U.S. government estimates, as cited by the author, how much oil is left in the ground?
2. As explained by Davy, what does Hubbert's formula say about oil production?
3. How much of the world's oil supply does the United States use, according to the author?

Emma Davy, "Crude Awakening: The World's Oil Supply Is Limited. How Much Is Left, and When Will It Run Out?" *Current Science*, vol. 90, March 4, 2004, pp. 4–7. Copyright © 2004 by the Weekly Reader Corporation. Reproduced by permission.

W hat do tires, tennis rackets, trash bags, and toothpaste have in common? They all start with the letter T, of course. They are also products made from "Texas tea"— crude oil, or liquid petroleum.

Oil is the single most important item traded between countries today. Ninety percent of the world's transportation runs on petroleum, and thousands of products—everything from drugs to detergents to fertilizers—are made from it. Less than 150 years after the world's first oil well was drilled on the shore of Oil Creek in Titusville, Pa., the global economy has been transformed.

Now another huge transformation is on the way. The world's available petroleum supplies are going to run out. Like the ages of stone, bronze, and iron before it, the age of oil will expire.

Peak Production

Exactly how much oil is left in the ground? No one knows for sure, but U.S. government scientists put the amount at about 2.6 trillion barrels. (One barrel is equal to 159 liters, or 42 gallons.) About 1.7 trillion barrels are "discovered" oil—oil that geologists have found but not yet pumped out. The remaining 900 billion barrels are "undiscovered" oil—oil that hasn't been found but that, theoretically, should be present in certain rock formations.

Now, 2.6 trillion barrels might seem like a lot of oil. But not all of it is there for the taking. In 1956, geophysicist M. King Hubbert introduced the concept of oil production peak. He observed that the flow of petroleum from any oil field climbs to a peak and then declines just as quickly. Once half the oil has been pumped out of the ground, the remaining half becomes harder and more expensive to extract. Production falls off and the field is eventually abandoned, leaving perhaps millions of barrels of oil in the ground and out of reach. Hubbert predicted that the oil pumped from U.S. fields would peak around 1970—and it did.

Using Hubbert's formula, world oil production will peak in about 2030, says Paul Roberts, author of the new book *The End of Oil.* After that, output will decline.

According to Roberts, who interviewed many geologists

Remaining Oil Reserves

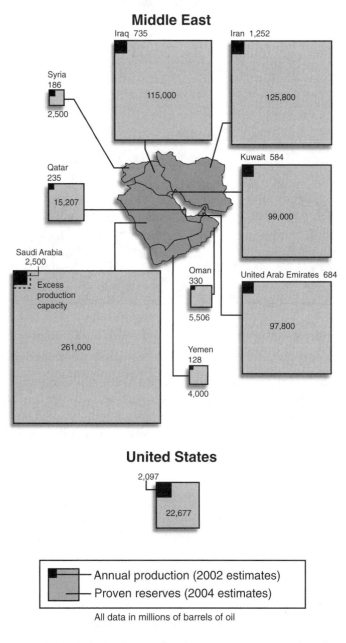

Middle East

Iraq 735
115,000

Iran 1,252
125,800

Syria
186
2,500

Qatar
235
15,207

Kuwait 584
99,000

Saudi Arabia
2,500
Excess
production
capacity
261,000

Oman
330
5,506

United Arab Emirates 684
97,800

Yemen
128
4,000

United States

2,097
22,677

Annual production (2002 estimates)
Proven reserves (2004 estimates)

All data in millions of barrels of oil

Source: *National Geographic*, 2004.

and economists for his book, the decline in oil production will not be the only problem. Drilling for new oil will also become much harder. As the last of what Roberts calls "easy oil" disappears, people will have to tap remote regions such as the frozen tundra of Siberia and the 3 kilometer-deep floor of the Caspian Sea.

Rothco. © by Al Liederman—Rothco Cartoons. Reproduced by permission.

That's not all. Remaining oil resources will also be difficult to process. The United States harbors two-thirds of the world's oil shale, a fine-grained sedimentary rock from which oil can be extracted. But oil shale is expensive to mine and takes huge amounts of water and heat to distill.

Political Turmoil

Another problem, says Roberts, is the division of the world into two groups of oil suppliers: OPEC and non-OPEC. OPEC stands for the Organization of Petroleum Exporting Countries and includes Algeria, Indonesia, Iran, Iraq, Kuwait, Libya, Nigeria, Qatar, Saudi Arabia, the United Arab Emirates, and Venezuela.

The OPEC-controlled Persian Gulf region in the Middle East has 65 percent of the world's oil, much of it in Saudi Arabia. Getting that oil has sometimes been difficult because war and political instability plague the Middle East. OPEC countries also limit their oil exports to keep prices up.

As a result, the energy-hungry West has relied heavily on non-OPEC oil, which has been depleted faster. Experts estimate that non-OPEC oil, which comes from places such as the Gulf of Mexico, the North Sea, Norway, and Russia, could peak as early as 2015. At that point, suggests Roberts, the United States and other countries will have to pay whatever price the OPEC countries demand for their oil.

Fueling Demands

Meanwhile, the world's thirst for petroleum intensifies. Oil already provides 40 percent of the world's energy. Fast-developing nations such as China and India are putting escalating demands on global supply. The U.S. economy is more energy efficient than it used to be (automobiles travel twice as far on a gallon of gas today as they did in 1970), but Americans continue to want bigger cars and homes. The United States has only 4 percent of Earth's population but guzzles about 25 percent of its oil supply. Roberts calls the United States "energy illiterate" because most Americans consider conserving energy only when faced with price hikes at the gas pumps.

Oil-Free Choices

What options should Americans pursue in the remaining years of the age of oil? Roberts's suggestions include
- doubling the fuel efficiency of cars by driving gas-electric hybrids;
- installing the most efficient heating, lighting, and cooling systems in buildings;
- increasing research into renewable energy sources, including solar, wind, and geothermal power. Renewable sources never run out or can be replaced by new growth. Developing those resources will take decades and trillions of dollars.

In the meantime, Roberts sees natural gas as a "bridge" fuel between dwindling oil supplies and undeveloped renewable energies. Natural gas is a clean-burning component of crude oil that often lies in separate underground deposits. Enormous natural gas fields in Iran, Qatar, Russia, and Turkmenistan could fuel the world for more than 50 years.

However, natural gas, like oil, is nonrenewable. The longer the world waits to turn to renewable forms of energy, says Roberts, the more devastating the change will be. "Oil depletion," he says, "is arguably the most serious crisis ever to face industrial society."

*"Depletionists-qua-alarmists err . . . by
neglecting the vast size of the estimated
carbon-energy resource base."*

America Can Safely Rely on Growing Oil Reserves

Robert L. Bradley Jr.

In the following viewpoint Robert L. Bradley Jr. argues against claims that the United States will run out of oil in the twenty-first century. Oil is not a finite resource, he argues, because human ingenuity can "grow" the supply. According to Bradley, as a result of future research and increasing knowledge about extraction and production, oil resources around the world will actually increase. Bradley is president of the Institute for Energy Research and a senior research fellow at the University of Houston, Texas. He is also coauthor of *Energy: The Master Resource.*

As you read, consider the following questions:

1. As explained by Bradley, what is the deflationist theory?
2. What is the expansionist theory, according to the author?
3. In Bradley's opinion, how were the 1970s oil price increases related to human factors rather than to depletion?

"**T**his time it's for real," says the cover story of the June 2004 issue of *National Geographic*. "We're at the beginning of the end of cheap oil."

Books and articles written by geologists, environmentalists, and others regularly announce a new era of increasing oil scarcity. Today's resurrected hero of the depletionists is M. King Hubbert (1903–1989), a Shell Oil Company geologist who a half century ago presented a bell-shaped curve depicting oil production over time. But the theory of a little-known twentieth-century economist, Erich Zimmermann, suggests this is unsound.

Hubbert's model correctly predicted that U.S. oil production would peak around 1970. A sister prediction, that U.S. gas production would peak in 1970, was errant, however. And his prediction that global oil production would begin an irreversible decline around 2000 is off to a poor start. World oil production in 2003 was about 2.5 percent above 2000.

The logic behind mineral-resource pessimism is simple. It goes like this: Oil is a finite resource, incapable of being reproduced in human time frames. Any usage reduces the stock, and geometric demand growth, such as the 1.9 percent annual increase in oil demand predicted for the next two decades, will rapidly deplete remaining supplies. Fixed supply plus rising demand equals depletion and increasing economic scarcity.

The Expansionist Theory

"But look at the data," expansionists respond. The resource base for different minerals has expanded tremendously over time to meet growing demand—and at steady, and even falling, prices when adjusted for inflation. Resource availability has been positively, not negatively, correlated to consumption when human ingenuity has been allowed free rein.

The expansionist position is often associated with Julian Simon, who in 1990 won the most famous wager in the history of economics. He bet [biologist] Paul Ehrlich, [energy expert] John Holdren, and others that the inflation-adjusted price of mineral resources would be less in 1990 than in 1980, and it was. A similar bet undertaken today would likely be a winner, too. Prices of global oil and North American

natural gas in recent years have been higher than their historical average, but supply and demand adjustments promise to bring these prices down over time—given access to reserves and entrepreneurial incentives.

Erich Zimmermann

The gulf between the depletionists and expansionists can be better understood—even resolved—by appreciating the insights of the functional theory of mineral resources developed by Erich Zimmermann (1888–1961), an economist at the University of North Carolina and later the University of Texas. His insight provides a theoretical foundation for modern expansionist thought.

Zimmermann rejected the assumption of fixity. Resources are not known, fixed things; they are what humans employ to service wants at a given time. To Zimmermann, only human "appraisal" turns the "neutral stuff" of the earth into resources. What are resources today may not be tomorrow, and vice versa.

"Resources are highly dynamic functional concepts; they are not, they become, they evolve out of the triune interaction of nature, man, and culture, in which nature sets outer limits, but man and culture are largely responsible for the portion of physical totality that is made available for human use". Zimmermann concluded that "knowledge is truly the mother of all resources".

Zimmermann drew a clear distinction between the ways in which natural scientists and social scientists view resources. "To the physicist the law of the conservation of matter and energy is basic. The economist, however, is less interested in the totality of the supply than in its availability". He warned: "To those who are used to viewing resources as material fixtures of physical nature, this functional interpretation of resources must seem disconcerting" since "it robs the resource concept of its concreteness and turns it into an elusive vapor".

The Problem with "Hard" Science

Physical to functional; objective to subjective; absolute to relative; static to dynamic; one-dimensional to institutional—Zimmermann's real-world theory was ignored by the eco-

nomic orthodoxy in its quest to remake their discipline into a "hard" science based on mathematical relationships. Economists embraced deterministic ideas of known, fixed resources that enabled them to calculate the "optimal" extraction rate of a "depletable" resource. But it was at the expense of understanding the dynamics of real-world resources.

A Pessimistic Mind-Set

Dire warnings about oil shortages have been around almost since oil wells were first drilled. In the late 1800s, the oil fields in the eastern U.S. were in decline, raising doubts about the possibility of providing for U.S. energy needs. The U.S. Geological Survey was founded at this time in part because of fears of oil shortages. Then the discovery, in 1897, of a single oil well in northeastern Oklahoma, the famous Nellie Johnstone #1, started the Oklahoma oil boom and temporarily ended any threat of an oil shortage. Even though past forecasts of oil crises have continually been proven wrong, there's no shortage of additional predictions of this sort.

Mark Brandly, 2004. www.mises.org.

Depletionists-qua-alarmists err on their own ground by neglecting the vast size of the estimated carbon-energy resource base. The World Energy Council has concluded that "fossil fuel resources are adequate to meet a wide range of possible scenarios through to 2050 . . . and well beyond." Similarly, the Intergovernmental Panel on Climate Change (IPCC) found that fossil fuels are so abundant that they "will not limit carbon emissions during the 21st century". The IPCC estimates that only about 1.5 percent of the total physical resource base of the Earth's crust was produced and consumed between 1860 and 1998. Such supply represents, potentially, many thousands of years of increasing consumption.

Geologists divide the earth's resource base into three categories: "proved" (found and ready to be produced), "probable" (expected to become proved in time), and "speculative" (estimated but uneconomic). Resourceship—that is, entrepreneurial development of resources—turns probable into proved, and speculative into probable. What is high cost today becomes lower cost tomorrow. Heavy oils, such as orimulsion in Venezuela and bitumen in Alberta, Canada, are

now rivals to crude oil. These are examples of Zimmermann's "resources are not, they become" that he did not live to see.

A New Paradigm

Vainly, economists working in the fixity paradigm have looked for a "depletion signal" in the empirical record—some definitive turning point at which physical scarcity overcomes human ingenuity. A new research program is in order. Applied economists should focus upon institutional change to explain and quantify changes in resource scarcity. The legal framework of a country, and even a people's customs, explain the abundance or paucity of mineral development.

The 1970s' price spikes with crude oil can be better understood in terms of human factors rather than as a depletion signal. Nature's "tank" was not running low; rather, government-imposed price ceilings distorted market processes. Similarly, today's high oil prices, at least in part, reflect an "institutional signal"—an artificial scarcity partly caused by the political blockage of oil production in the Arctic National Wildlife Refuge in Alaska and other technologically producible oil provinces around the world.

Resources grow with improving knowledge, expanding capital, and capitalistic policies, including privatization of the subsoil, that encourage market entrepreneurship. Resources shrink with war, revolution, strife, nationalization, taxation, price controls, and access restrictions. Man is the creator of resources, but man can also destroy and immobilize resources.

Whether or not oil, gas, and coal are exploited far into the future depends not only on consumer demand but also on whether government policies will allow the ultimate resource of human ingenuity to turn the "neutral stuff" of the earth into resources in ever-better ways. With this understanding, it may be appropriate to join energy economist M.A. Adelman and abandon the term "exhaustible" to describe mineral resources. The end of the misleading renewable-nonrenewable framework would bring Zimmermann's functional theory to full flower and improve understanding for better real-world decision making.

"The United States refuses to stop hogging resources."

The American Lifestyle Is Destroying the Environment

Derrick Z. Jackson

The United States consumes resources at an unsustainable rate, argues Derrick Z. Jackson in the following viewpoint, which accelerates the destruction of the global environment. While other countries have taken steps to improve their environmental stewardship, says Jackson, the United States refuses to reduce its resource consumption or to use its technological know-how to reduce pollution. Jackson was a 2001 finalist for the Pulitzer Prize in political commentary and a winner of commentary awards from the National Education Writers Association.

As you read, consider the following questions:

1. As stated by Jackson, out of 146 nations, where does the United States rank for protecting the environment?
2. How many other nations and economic groups have signed the Kyoto agreement on global warming, according to the author?
3. According to Jackson, how did other countries react to bad rankings in a 2002 report on environmental stewardship?

Derrick Z. Jackson, "Neglecting Mother Earth," *Boston Globe*, January 26, 2005. Copyright © 2005 by the *Boston Globe*. Reproduced by permission of Copyright Clearance Center.

L ocal insanity plus global inanity adds up to an embarrassing American moment.

Last week [February 2005], a 37-year-old man in a caffeine craze parked his Hummer in a loading zone in Boston's Back Bay. By the time he rushed in and out of Starbucks, a meter maid was writing out a ticket. The driver was so outraged, he allegedly threw the scalding cup at the meter maid. She got first-degree burns on her face. The man said he merely slipped on the ice. Police so far believe the meter maid and charged him with assault with a deadly weapon.

Irresponsible Stewardship

This week, researchers at Yale and Columbia, in collaboration with the World Economic Forum, published its latest index of global environmental stewardship. Out of 146 nations, the United States, the world's richest nation, ranked only 45th for protecting the environment.

This is even more ridiculous based on who is ahead of us. The United States, with a [per capita] gross domestic product [GDP] of $37,800, according to the CIA [Central Intelligence Agency] *World Handbook*, trails Gabon, Peru, Paraguay, Costa Rica, Bolivia, Colombia, Albania, Central African Republic, Panama, Namibia, Russia, Botswana, Papua New Guinea, Malaysia, Congo, Mali, Chile, Bhutan, and Armenia. Those 19 nations all have [per capita] GDPs of under $10,000, going as low as Bhutan's $1,300, the Central African Republic's $1,100, Mali's $900, and Congo's $700. The average American has 54 times more money in GDP terms than the average person in Congo. Yet the Congolese exhibit better stewardship of the planet.

An angry man in one of America's largest gas-guzzling cars in one of the most chronically congested parts of the city throws some of the nation's most expensive coffee at a working-class woman.

At the same time, we receive yet more evidence [of] how we blow smoke in the face of the world with our pollution and refuse to join the other 136 nations and regional economic groups that signed the international Kyoto agreement on global warming [to reduce global emissions of carbon dioxide and other greenhouse gases]. The incivility at

home and arrogance abroad makes for one ugly American.

On environmental stewardship, it is easy to forget that in the 1970s, the United States led the world in cleaning up air pollution, said Marc Levy, associate director of Columbia University's Center for International Earth Science Information Network, one of the authors of the 2005 Environmental Sustainability Index. "Europe was way behind us," Levy said over the telephone. . . . "Our big advance in the '70s was clear targets on air quality, with incentives and punishments, putting catalytic converters in cars and smokestack scrubbers in industrial plants. But we pretty much stopped there. In the past 10 years, Europe has passed us and we're 50 percent below most countries over there on average."

No Efforts to Improve

Levy said that Europe has vaulted past us with far more strategic efforts to promote rail transportation, reduce coal burning, and recycling solid waste, all of which are stifled in the United States by special-interest lobbying that turns politicians into cowards and wrongfully convinces working-class workers that less pollution means less jobs.

"There is absolutely no reason we cannot move to levels other countries have already shown to be possible," Levy said. "We don't have to keep filling landfills and churning up the incinerators the way we do.

"The striking thing on the positive side is that we're still not only the world leader but remain far ahead of the rest of the world in the science and technology available to us. If we put our resources to work effectively, we may not only get our own house in order but help alleviate things globally."

Five years ago, poor standings in a pilot version of the index sparked a cabinet-level review of environmental practices in Mexico. In 2002, bad rankings moved the governments of South Korea, the United Arab Emirates, the Philippines, and Belgium to also conduct policy reviews.

Those nations, Levy said, took the index as a "slap in the face." So far, Levy said, the United States under the Bush administration has shown no interest in the index.

Enslaving the Planet

Stewardship, as defined by Bush, was taking a draft report by the Environmental Protection Agency and deleting the part that specifically mentioned vehicle exhaust and industrial pollution as major factors in global warming. In his second inaugural address, Bush talked at length about spreading liberty throughout the world. We can grant no liberty when we enslave the planet to our consumption.

The United States refuses to stop hogging resources. A man in a giant car in a dense neighborhood refuses to accept the result of hogging an illegal space. The United States leads the world in heating up the planet. The man burns a woman's face. Globally and locally, we are creating a fiery place.

> *"The gains in environmental progress and resource abundance are a result of the most precious resource of all: the human intellect."*

America Does Not Face an Environmental Crisis

Stephen Moore

In the following viewpoint Stephen Moore insists that, contrary to popular opinion, America's environment is not in crisis, and is, in fact, healthier than in years past. Reports show that in the past fifty years, America's air has become less polluted, its water has become cleaner, and its forests have expanded, says Moore. He explains that America is not depleting its natural resources such as forests and clean water; instead, as knowledge expands and technology improves, America's natural resources are actually expanding. Moore is president of the Club for Growth, a Washington, D.C.–based policy organization, and a contributing editor for *National Review*.

As you read, consider the following questions:

1. What does a reduction in waterborne diseases in the United States mean, according to the author?
2. According to the Forest Service, as cited by Moore, by what percentage are U.S. forests increasing every year?
3. In the author's opinion, what would happen if the United States was not creating more resources than it uses up?

Stephen Moore, "Is Pollution in America Getting Worse?" *Vision & Values*, vol. 10, March 2002. Copyright © 2001 by *Vision & Values*. Reproduced by permission.

There is almost certainly no issue of modern times in which Americans' general beliefs about the state of affairs is so contrary to objective reality than in the area of the environment. Most Americans believe that because of industrialization, population growth and mass consumption, our air and our water are deteriorating and that our access to natural resources will soon run dry. We read stories about global warming, ozone depletion, and the paving over of the planet and think that the environment must have been cleaner and more pristine 50 and 100 years ago.

In a recent poll, when Americans were asked what would be some of the greatest problems that mankind will confront over the next 50 years, the top two responses dealt with the environment. More than four of five said they feared "severe water pollution" and "severe air pollution" with three areas of environmental conditions: 1) air quality, 2) water quality and 3) availability of natural resources.

The Reality

But here is the real state of the environment. Contrary to infamous doom and gloom reports of the 1960s and 1970s, we are not running out of energy, food, forests or minerals. The data clearly show that natural resource scarcity—as measured by cost or price—has been decreasing rather than increasing in the long run for all raw materials, energy and food, with only temporary exceptions. That is, resources have become more abundant, not less so. Even the U.S. government now apparently recognizes the errors of its judgments in the past. Reversing the forecasts of studies such as Global 2000, the Office of Technology Assessment in *Technology and the American Transition* has concluded: "The nation's future has probably never been less constrained by the cost of natural resources."

The major driving forces behind our improved environment are our greater access to natural resources, our affluence and our technology. Technological improvements and inventions have helped combat the worst kinds of pollution. The computer, for example, is arguably the most environmentally friendly invention in world history, by producing massive amounts of output with virtually no environmental costs. It is also true that a wealthier society is a healthier one. Wealthier societies can afford to devote more resources to combating pollution. We now know that the greatest environmental catastrophes of this century were caused by socialist nations. The Communists in the Soviet Union were perhaps the greatest environmental villains in history. Prudent government regulation is necessary to protect the environment. But more important is a free market economy: one that protects property rights, produces wealth and encourages innovation. . . .

Measuring Air Quality

But let us look at more direct evidence on the amount of air pollution in the U.S. The prevailing attitude of Americans, amplified by the media and academia, is that the giant leaps forward in industrial production have come at the expense of degrading our air and water quality. In the 1960s Harvard economist John Kenneth Galbraith wrote in his bestseller, *The Affluent Society*, that a fundamental tension exists between environmental and economic progress. Former Vice President Al Gore wrote more contemporaneously in his book, *Earth in the Balance*, that we have been mortgaging our environmental future through our mindless pursuit of economic growth. The surprising good news is that the economic progress of the last century has not come at the expense of clean air. Rather, economic growth has generally corresponded with improvements in the natural environment.

The national picture on air quality shows improvement for almost every type of pollution. Lead concentrations have amazingly fallen by more than 90 percent since 1976. In fact, the total volume of lead emissions was lower in 1990 than in 1940 (the furthest back we have reliable data) and was lower than in every intervening year. According to a 1999 report by the Pacific Research Institute, based on EPA [Environmental Protection Agency] air quality data, between 1976 and 1998 sulfur dioxide levels decreased 66 percent, nitrogen oxides decreased 38 percent, ozone decreased 31 percent, carbon monoxide decreased 66 percent, and particulates decreased 25 percent (between 1988 and 1997).

What about the smog levels in particular high-pollution

Breathe Easy

America's air has become a great deal cleaner over the last generation. Since measurement began in 1970, U.S. emissions have fallen dramatically, even while GDP [gross domestic product] and travel have more than doubled. America, in other words, is producing much more while polluting less.

Ambient air pollution levels
1976–2001

Ozone	–33%
Sulfur Dioxides	–67%
Nitrogen Dioxide	–42%
Carbon Monoxide	–73%
Particulates *	–27%
Lead	–97%

Note: * 1996–2001

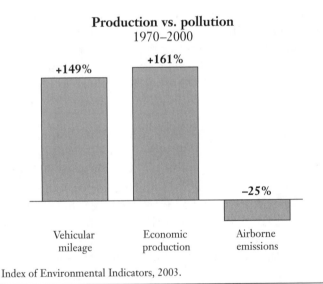

Production vs. pollution
1970–2000

+149% Vehicular mileage

+161% Economic production

–25% Airborne emissions

Index of Environmental Indicators, 2003.

cities? It was just a bit over 30 years ago that doomsayer [biologist] Paul Ehrlich wrote in *The Population Bomb*, that "smog disasters" might kill 200,000 people in New York or Los Angeles by 1973. The reality is that air pollution in American cities has been falling for at least the past three decades. For example, air pollution, or soot, over Manhattan has fallen by two-thirds since the end of World War II. Air pollution over Chicago, Denver, Philadelphia and Washington, D.C., declined by more than 50 percent between 1972 and 1996. Perhaps the most gratifying environmental success story in recent years has been the rapid reduction in smog levels over Los Angeles in just the past decade. From 1985 to 1995, the number of days in the year of unhealthy air quality has fallen from about 160 to about 80. Pittsburgh's air quality improvements over the past 40 years have been even more spectacular. In the 1920s, 30s, 40s and 50s, as the steel mills' smokestacks belched out black soot, there were typically more than 300 "smoky" days a year. Since the late 1960s, that number has fallen to about 60 smoky days a year.

Water Quality Trends

One measure of the improvement in water quality over this century has been the dramatic reduction in outbreaks of disease from drinking water. At the start of the century, many life-threatening illnesses, such as diarrhea, were a result of Americans drinking and using impure water. In fact, waterborne diseases were a leading cause of death in the nineteenth century. In the 1930s and 1940s there were about 25 waterborne disease outbreaks a year. Nowadays there are almost none.

Unfortunately, there is not much reliable long-term data on the pollution levels of American lakes and rivers. Official measurements come from the Environmental Protection Agency and start around 1960—a decade or so before the Clean Water Act was signed into law. Over the past quarter century our lakes, streams and rivers have become much less polluted, and the trend is toward continued improvement. Since 1970 an estimated $500 billion has been spent on water cleanup. That spending has apparently paid off. The percentage of water sources that were judged by the Council on Environmental Quality to be poor or severe fell from 30 percent in 1961 to 17 percent in 1974 to less than 5 percent today.

We have made huge progress in purifying industrial and municipal waste before it is emitted into streams, rivers, and lakes. In 1960 only 40 million Americans—22 percent of the population—were served by wastewater treatment plants. By 1996 that had risen to 190 million Americans, or 72 percent of the population. One consequence of these gains is that many streams, rivers and lakes which were at one time severely polluted are now much more pristine. . . .

Lost Land and Trees

We sometimes hear it said that economic progress in the United States has come at the expense of one of our most treasured national assets: our land. Suburbanization and increasing population is said to be imperiling our ability to feed ourselves in the future as we pave hundreds of thousands of additional acres in concrete every year. From 1960 to 1990 the number of acres classified as "urban land" has more than doubled from 25 million to 56 million. Yet the percentage of land in the United States that is devoted to urban/suburban use is only about three percent of the total land area of the continent. The rate at which land is being converted to suburban development is about 0.0006 percent per year, which is hardly a worrisome trend. In fact, lands protected from development have outpaced urban land conversion over recent decades.

While there may be some cause for concern about preserving tropical rain forests in Brazil and other developing nations, the U.S. forests are not shrinking. Currently, the Forest Service reports that the U.S. is growing about 22 million net new cubic feet of wood a year and harvesting only 16.5 million—a net increase of 36 percent per year. This contrasts with the situation in the early years of this century, where about twice as many trees were cut as were planted.

The Knowledge to Improve the Environment

The evidence presented above shows that, on average, Americans of each generation create a bit more than they use up. Not only must this be true to account for the increase in our wealth and numbers, but if this were not so—if we used up a bit more than we create, and our assets deteriorated—we simply would have become extinct as a species. The essential condition of fitness for survival of our species is that each generation creates a net surplus on average, or at least breaks even. Since we have survived and increased, this condition must have been present. The question then immediately arises: Must not we, like other species, cease our growth when we have filled up our niche—that is, reached the limit of the available resources? One cannot answer this question with assurance, of course, because with each increase of wealth and numbers, we proceed into a situation with which we have no prior experience.

But as can be seen in the evidence of the increasing availability of natural resources throughout history as measured by their declining prices—especially food, metals and energy—there apparently is no fixed limit on our resources in the future. There are limits at any moment, but the limits continually expand, and constrain us less with each passing generation.

All of this is to say that the gains in environmental progress and resource abundance are a result of the most precious resource of all: the human intellect. This is the primary reason that we should be optimistic that the gains that have been made in the past 100 years will continue in the twenty-first century rather than reverse themselves. This is because almost all of the progress noted in the previous sections is primarily the result of the wondrous advances in the storehouse of human knowledge that has accumulated in this century.

We now stand on the shoulders of our ancestors, able to draw upon the accumulated knowledge and know-how of the past two centuries. This knowledge is our communal wealth. Much more than the power to enjoy gadgets, our wealth represents the power to mobilize nature to our advantage, rather than to just accept the random fates of nature. We now have all the evidence at hand to say definitively that Malthus[1] was wrong, and so were his legions of modern-day doomsday followers.

---

1. In 1784 economist Thomas Malthus predicted that the world's population would eventually outgrow its food supply.

"[Nuclear] technology is capable of providing lower cost, safe energy in virtually infinite amounts."

Nuclear Power Can Be Used to Meet America's Energy Requirements

Tom Solon

The United States needs to reduce its use of fossil fuels and increase its use of nuclear power, argues engineer and nuclear power advocate Tom Solon in the following viewpoint. Solon believes nuclear power is cheap, safe, and virtually infinite. Fears of nuclear accidents have deterred the use of this technology, he says, but these fears are unjustified. In Solon's opinion, nuclear power plants are safer than ever before because of tight regulations.

As you read, consider the following questions:

1. What examples does Solon give of the negative effects of fossil fuels on the environment?
2. According to the author, how do the risks from nuclear power compare to the risks of fossil fuels?
3. What types of risks do people take every day, as argued by Solon?

Tom Solon, "It's All About Power: Nuclear Energy Should Be Our Main Power Source," *Design News*, vol. 60, February 21, 2005, p. 16. Copyright © 2005 by Reed Business Information. Reproduced by permission.

Engineers know it all. At parties, after everyone has given their opinion, everyone asks the engineer to tell them the real answer. Engineers deal in facts, data, and probabilities. And engineers are trusted. The public may have lost trust in the medical profession, in our leaders, and in our favorite news reporters. But, though they make jokes about us, engineers are viewed as straight shooters. This trust gives us power. It also carries responsibility.

Our nation, our world, is in a crisis, a crisis of power. Specifically, our dependency on fossil fuels has the world at war. Regardless of one's politics, it is an irrefutable fact that oil drives much of our economy and has fueled many of the recent wars. The sad truth is that we have a solution that we are not using.

A Low-Cost, Safe Alternative

Nuclear energy is the answer. Current technology is capable of providing lower cost, safe energy in virtually infinite amounts. And the prospect of commercially viable fusion reactors is closer than most believe. But the public has shut nuclear power down based on myth and fear.

We all know the list: Three Mile Island, Chernobyl, *The China Syndrome* (great movie, bad science),[1] radioactive waste, and worst of all, that link between nuclear power and the atom bomb.

But, fossil fuels, both oil and coal, have killed and continue to kill every day. Coal mine disasters, black lung, acid rain, hydrocarbon emissions, oil spills, poisoned water and land, oil platform disasters, refinery accidents, the Gulf War, and arguably most fighting in the Middle East are directly attributable to our dependence on fossil fuels. Add to this the economic risks of a world economy inextricably linked to oil, and our current concerns about terrorism (think refinery or LNG [liquefied natural gas] tanker explosions), and it is hard to understand why we are willing to use oil and gas at all.

1. In 1979 the Three Mile Island nuclear power station in Pennsylvania suffered a partial meltdown. In 1986 the Chernobyl nuclear power plant in the Ukraine was the site of the worst nuclear plant accident in history, contaminating the air and land for miles around. *The China Syndrome* movie was released after the Three Mile Island accident and attempted to raise public awareness about the risks of nuclear power.

Exaggerated Fears

Is nuclear energy perfect? Of course not. But let's give it some time. At its worst, it has been much safer and it is in its infancy. The potential is even more hopeful with the possibility of fusion and improved processes. We live in a world of managed risks. If you look at the scorecard, the risks from nuclear power cannot match the real, proven and ever increasing dangers we accept with fossil fuels. But the public's ongoing fear of radioactivity has paralyzed us. . . .

An "Eco-Efficient" Technology

Of all energy sources, nuclear energy has perhaps the lowest impact on the environment, especially in relation to kilowatts produced, because nuclear plants do not emit harmful gases, require a relatively small area, and effectively mitigate other impacts. In other words, nuclear energy is the most "eco-efficient" of all energy sources because it produces the most electricity in relation to its minimal environmental impact. There are no significant adverse effects to water, land, habitat, species and air resources.

Nuclear Energy Institute, 2005.

People willingly inhale concentrated carcinogens (tobacco smoke), ingest poison (alcohol and others), subject themselves to all kinds of electromagnetic radiation (TV, cell phones, microwave ovens, power lines) and seek out powerful sources of ultraviolet radiation (tanning booths and sunlight). Yet we have managed to shut down the most tightly regulated industry ever to have existed (nuclear power).

Time for a Change

It is time to change this. We as engineers have the power, the public's trust. We need to tell the world that the emperor is naked! Look at the facts and decide for yourself. Then tell people what you have found. Write letters to your representatives and vote accordingly. Invest in companies that are developing nuclear energy. Explode the myth!

Or don't. But don't complain that you can't change things. Remember that it is your choice, your responsibility. Because you've got the power.

> "*Nuclear power is not a responsible choice.
> . . . We can meet our energy needs and
> have a clean and healthy world without
> nuclear power.*"

Nuclear Power Is Expensive and Unsafe

Dan Becker

In the following viewpoint Dan Becker maintains that nuclear technology is not a good way to provide for America's energy needs. Not only do nuclear reactors pose the risk of catastrophic accidents, he explains, but they also generate waste that is dangerous to human health and difficult to store. In addition, says Becker, nuclear power is a very expensive way to generate electricity. Becker is director of the Sierra Club's Global Warming and Energy Program.

As you read, consider the following questions:

1. How much waste does a nuclear reactor generate every year, according to the author?
2. As argued by Becker, in what two ways are taxpayers subsidizing the nuclear industry?
3. According to the author, why are accidents at nuclear plants likely to occur?

Dan Becker, "Idea House," www.ncpa.org, 2001. Copyright © 2001 by the National Center for Policy Analysis. Reproduced by permission.

P resident [George W.] Bush has made the mistake of proposing that the United States expand its nuclear energy industry.

Generating electricity from nuclear sources poses at least four insurmountable problems: the production of highly dangerous radioactive waste, a prohibitively high cost, the potential for accidents and the risk of nuclear weapons proliferation.

Nuclear Waste

First, every nuclear reactor generates about 20 tons of highly radioactive spent nuclear fuel and additional low-level radioactive waste per year.

Radioactive waste is one of the most dangerous materials known to humankind—it can kill at high doses and cause cancer and birth defects at low doses. Nuclear waste remains dangerous to humans for 200 thousand years.

Worse, we don't know what to do with this waste once it is generated. The nuclear industry and some in Congress propose dumping nuclear waste in Yucca Mountain, NV; however, the mountain is seismically active.

An earthquake in the 1990's caused over $1 million damage to a Department of Energy (DOE) facility at the site. In addition, a DOE panel of scientists has found that the nuclear material may leak from the containment vessels over time and will contaminate groundwater.

On its way to Yucca Mountain, the waste will pass through thousands of cities and towns. There are serious concerns about the exposure risks in transporting the waste from all over the country into Nevada.

An Expensive Industry

Second, nuclear power is the most expensive way ever devised to generate electricity. The method is not anywhere near cost effective; nuclear plants in the states of Oregon, New Jersey, Maine, Illinois, and Connecticut have been shut down before the end of their planned lives because the owners found it was too expensive to keep them going.

American taxpayers are subsidizing the nuclear industry. According to the Congressional Research Service, the indus-

An Expensive Energy Source

At present [2005] there are 442 nuclear reactors in operation around the world. If, as the nuclear industry suggests, nuclear power were to replace fossil fuels on a large scale, it would be necessary to build 2000 large, 1000-megawatt reactors. Considering that no new nuclear plant has been ordered in the US since 1978, this proposal is less than practical. Furthermore, even if we decided today to replace all fossil-fuel-generated electricity with nuclear power, there would only be enough economically viable uranium to fuel the reactors for three to four years.

The true economies of the nuclear industry are never fully accounted for. The cost of uranium enrichment is subsidised by the US government. The true cost of the industry's liability in the case of an accident in the US is estimated to be $US 560 billion, but the industry pays only $US 9.1 billion—98 per cent of the insurance liability is covered by the US federal government. The cost of decommissioning all the existing US nuclear reactors is estimated to be $US 33 billion. These costs—plus the enormous expense involved in the storage of radioactive waste for a quarter of a million years—are not now included in the economic assessments of nuclear electricity.

Helen Caldicott, *Australian*, April 15, 2005.

try has cost taxpayers $66 billion in research and development subsidies.

When no private insurer would underwrite the risks inherent to a nuclear plant, Congress passed the Price-Anderson law, which provides taxpayer-subsidized insurance.

Accidents

Third is the danger of an accident. An accident at a coal plant is a problem. An accident at a nuclear plant can be a disaster. Because human beings operate plants and drive the trucks that transport nuclear waste, accidents can and will happen.

The danger with nuclear power is that the stakes in accidents are extremely high. Anyone exposed to radiation leaks or accidents will likely sicken or die from that exposure.

Cleanup costs will be in the billions. Public Citizen [advocacy organization] has found that more than 90 percent of the country's reactors have been in violation of government safety regulations during the last three years, potentially increasing the risk of accidents.

An Irresponsible Choice

Finally, there is the risk that nuclear material will fall into the wrong hands. President Bush has recommended that we consider [the] "reprocessing" of spent nuclear fuel, a method that consolidates waste into weapons-usable plutonium. The government has elaborate plants to prevent rogue nations and terrorists from stealing the nuclear fuel or waste to make nuclear bombs. The more nuclear reactors, the more risk of radioactive material being stolen to make bombs.

Nuclear power is not a responsible choice. We can meet our energy needs through energy efficiency, renewable energy like solar and wind power, and responsible additions to supply. We can meet our energy needs and have a clean and healthy world without nuclear power. America deserves a safer, cleaner, and cheaper energy future.

Periodical Bibliography

The following articles have been selected to supplement the diverse views presented in this chapter.

Frank Ackerman	"Is the United States a Pollution Haven?" *Dollars & Sense*, March/April 2003.
M.A. Adelman	"The Real Oil Problem," *Regulation*, Spring 2004.
Tony Clarke and Maude Barlow	"The Battle for Water," *Yes!* Winter 2004.
Roy Cordato	"'The State of the Air': Propaganda, Not Science," *Ideas on Liberty*, October 2003.
John D'Aloia Jr.	"Energy Matters," *St. Croix Review*, October 2003.
Alisa Gravitz	"Solar's Moment in the Sun," *Liberal Opinion Week*, May 31, 2004.
David Helvarg	"Coasts at Risk," *Multinational Monitor*, September 2003.
Marya Hillesland	"Creating Policies That Promote a Healthy Global Society," *Friends Journal*, October 2004.
Michael Klare	"No Escape from Foreign Oil Dependency," *Human Quest*, January/February 2005.
Thomas P. Lyon	"'Green' Firms Bearing Gifts," *Regulation*, Fall 2003.
David Pimental and Marcia Pimental	"Land, Energy, and Water," *Social Contract*, Summer 2002.
Jordan E. Powell	"After the Oil Runs Out," *Liberal Opinion Week*, June 21, 2004.
Charley Reese	"Myth of Independence," *Conservative Chronicle*, June 23, 2004.
Glenn Carroll Strait	"If We Can't Quench Our Thirst," *World & I*, June 2003.
William Tucker	"The Solution," *American Enterprise*, January/February 2005.
Robin Weissman	"Precaution and Power," *Multinational Monitor*, September 2004.

CHAPTER 2

What Role Will Technology Play in America's Future?

Chapter Preface

As the United States moves into the twenty-first century, numerous technological advances are invoking both hope and fear. One of these advances is the use of genetic engineering to create human organs for transplant. In 2005 more than eighty thousand people in the United States were waiting for lifesaving organ transplants. The number of available organs, however, was far less than needed, and in that same year, thousands of people died without receiving the liver, kidney, or heart they desperately needed. Some people believe that genetic engineering technology can be used to increase the number of organs available for transplant. Many experts believe that scientists will learn to genetically alter animal organs to be accepted by the human body. Others believe headless human clones will be used to grow extra organs to be used for transplants. As scientists learn more about human genetics, controversy about how genetic engineering will impact society is sure to grow. Genetic engineering is just one of the many technologies that will impact America's future. In addition to genetically altering human organs, other important genetic engineering technologies include human cloning and the development of genetically modified food.

Some people believe genetic engineering can dramatically improve the lives of Americans. According to researchers Henry I. Miller and Gregory Conko, this technology has led to the development of lifesaving medicines and improvements in agriculture that have greatly enhanced human life. "So powerful is [biotechnology]," they maintain, "that literally tens of millions of lives worldwide have been protected, enriched, and even lengthened due to these techniques." Biotechnology advocates such as Miller and Conko dismiss fears of genetically engineered foods and medicines as simply an unfounded "scare-mongering campaign." According to biotechnology advocate Peter Cresswell, "Technology's attackers litter their statements with arbitrary attacks full of 'might be,' and 'could-be,' and 'could-lead-to,'" but have no real proof that genetic engineering is, or will be, harmful in any way.

However, while numerous commentators support genetic engineering, many analysts contend that this technology will negatively impact society. Ronnie Cummins, director of the Organic Consumers Association, warns, "The reality . . . of the Biotech Century that lies ahead is frightening. Genetic engineering poses unprecedented ethical and social concerns, as well as serious challenges to the environment, human health, animal welfare, and the future of agriculture." As an example, Cummins discusses genetic engineering of babies, and how this may lead to the devaluing of human life. If we can control the genetics of our babies, "will we abort fetuses on the basis of non-life threatening impairments," he wonders, "or for purely cosmetic reasons?" Physician Leon R. Kass fears that genetic engineering is proceeding without regard to potentially negative consequences such as the commoditization of human life. "Even the more modest biogenic engineers . . . are in the immortality business," he warns, "proceeding on the basis of a quasi-religious faith that all innovation is by definition progress, no matter what is sacrificed to attain it."

The extent to which genetic engineering should be pursued by society remains a controversial topic in the United States. The authors in the following chapter examine this and other controversies surrounding the impact of technology on twenty-first-century America.

"The genetically engineered food products on the U.S. market today are as safe as their conventionally bred counterparts."

Genetically Engineered Foods Will Benefit Americans

Linda Bren

Genetic engineering can help scientists create foods that are far more beneficial to consumers than are conventional foods, argues Linda Bren in the following viewpoint. According to Bren, scientists may one day create plants that are more resistant to disease, foods that are free of allergens and more nutritious, and even plants that contain lifesaving pharmaceuticals. She maintains that genetically engineered foods are, and always will be, subject to extensive and thorough testing to prove their safety before they are permitted to be sold for human consumption. Bren is a contributor to *FDA Consumer*, the official magazine of the U.S. Food and Drug Administration.

As you read, consider the following questions:

1. According to the author, what three government agencies regulate genetically engineered plants?
2. As explained by Bren, what type of expert does the Food and Drug Administration employ to test the safety of genetically engineered foods?
3. What percentage of children aged six and under have food allergies, according to the author?

Linda Bren, "Genetic Engineering: The Future of Foods?" *FDA Consumer*, November/December 2003.

Hawaiian farmers were in trouble. In the mid-1990s, an insect-borne virus—the papaya ring spot virus (PRSV) —threatened to decimate Hawaii's second-largest fruit crop. Plant breeders scrambled to produce a virus-resistant papaya. When traditional plant breeding methods failed, researchers turned to genetic engineering.

Years of research were finally met with success, and by spring of 1998, Hawaiian farmers were planting the seeds of PRSV-resistant papaya.

Saving the Papaya Industry

"The results were dramatic," says Dennis Gonsalves, Ph.D., a Cornell University plant pathologist who led the researchers' efforts to save the tropical delicacy and the livelihood of Hawaii's growers. "It was not a matter of increasing the yield, but a matter of whether they could grow it or not grow it."

Gonsalves' team of researchers from academia, industry, and government had isolated and copied a virus gene, then used a device called a gene gun to "shoot" the gene into the cells of the papaya plant. The virus gene in the plant works somewhat like immunization, but the mechanism of resistance is different, says Gonsalves, now director of the U.S. Department of Agriculture's Pacific Basin Agricultural Research Center in Hilo, Hawaii. "By integrating this virus gene into the chromosomes of the papaya, this made the papaya and subsequent generations resistant to the virus."

The rescue of the Hawaiian papaya industry is "a really satisfying story," says Gonsalves, and one that shows the difference that genetic engineering can make in people's lives.

But not all share Gonsalves' enthusiasm for genetically engineered foods. Although the newness of these foods may be wearing off, public concern about the safety and environmental impact of genetically engineered foods remains.

Some consumers and advocacy groups urge mandatory labeling that discloses the use of genetic engineering. Others advocate more stringent testing of these products before marketing. Still others want a ban on all genetically engineered foods.

"The Food and Drug Administration [FDA] is confident

that the genetically engineered food products on the U.S. market today are as safe as their conventionally bred counterparts, and the agency is prepared to meet the safety and regulatory challenges presented by new products as they emerge from the laboratory," says Commissioner of Food and Drugs Mark B. McClellan, M.D., Ph.D. "Genetically engineered foods must adhere to the same high standards of safety under the Federal Food, Drug, and Cosmetic Act that apply to more traditional food products," McClellan adds.

Top Three Genetically Engineered Crops in the United States, 2003

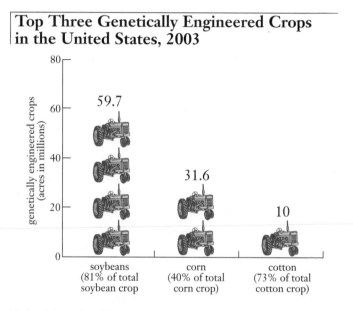

National Agricultural Statistics Service, U.S. Department of Agriculture, 2003.

Genetically engineered foods are produced from crops whose genetic makeup has been altered through a process called recombinant DNA, or gene splicing, to give the plant a desirable trait. Genetically engineered foods are also known as biotech, bioengineered, and genetically modified, although "genetically modified" can also refer to foods from plants altered through other breeding methods, says James Maryanski, Ph.D., the FDA's food biotechnology coordinator. "Scientists and farmers have been genetically modifying plants for hundreds of years," he says. Hybrid corn and tangelos (hybrid of a tangerine and grapefruit), for example, are the result of genetic modification through traditional methods of plant breeding. And the many varieties of apples we eat today were produced through genetic modification.

Using traditional genetic modification methods, such as cross-fertilization, scientists can produce a desired trait, such as a hardier plant. But in doing so, they mix thousands of genes from several plants, requiring many attempts over many years to weed out the unwanted traits that occur.

Newer methods of genetic modification, in the form of genetic engineering, are more precise and predictable—and faster. By controlling the insertion of one or two genes into a plant, scientists can give it a specific new characteristic without transferring undesirable traits. . . .

The Grocery Manufacturers of America estimates that between 70 percent and 75 percent of all processed foods available in U.S. grocery stores may contain ingredients from genetically engineered plants. Breads, cereal, frozen pizzas, hot dogs and soda are just a few of them.

Soybean oil, cottonseed oil and corn syrup are ingredients used extensively in processed foods. Soybeans, cotton and corn dominate the 100 million acres of genetically engineered crops that were planted in the United States in 2003, according to the U.S. Department of Agriculture (USDA). Through genetic engineering, these plants have been made to ward off pests and to tolerate herbicides used to kill weeds. Other crops, such as squash, potatoes, and papaya, have been engineered to resist plant diseases.

Safety of Genetically Engineered Foods

Genetically engineered plants are regulated by three government agencies: the FDA, the USDA, and the Environmental Protection Agency (EPA). The FDA ensures that foods made from these plants are safe for humans and animals to eat, the USDA makes sure the plants are safe to grow, and the EPA ensures that pesticides introduced into the plants are safe for human and animal consumption and for the environment. While these agencies act independently, they have a close working relationship since many products come under the review of all three.

The Federal Food, Drug, and Cosmetic Act (FD&C Act) gives the FDA authority to regulate foods for humans and animals, including foods derived from bioengineered plants. Under the act, companies have a legal obligation to ensure that any food they sell meets the safety standards of the law. The safety standards apply equally to conventional food and genetically engineered food. If a food does not meet the safety standards, the FDA has the authority to take it off the market.

Bioengineered foods do not pose any risks for consumers that are different from conventional foods, says Maryanski. "We make sure there are no hazards, such as an unexpected allergen or poisonous substance in the food, or that the food is not changed in some way that would affect its nutritional value."

The FDA's efforts to ensure the safety of bioengineered foods include publishing rigorous safety testing guidelines, establishing a consultation process with industry, and seeking the expertise of scientists outside the agency.

In 1992, the FDA published a policy statement and testing guidelines for foods developed using all methods of plant breeding, including the use of genetic engineering. These guidelines explain the types of food safety questions that developers should address in evaluating the safety of all plant-derived foods.

In 1994, the FDA set up a consultation process to assist developers in meeting the safety standards set forth in its guidelines. FDA scientists advise companies on the tests needed to assess the safety of new foods. After testing is completed, companies send safety and nutritional information to the FDA for the agency's scientific evaluation.

Although consultation is voluntary on the part of developers, the legal requirements that the foods have to meet are not. Some consumer advocates and scientists have urged the FDA to make the consultation process mandatory, but the agency believes that companies are cooperating within the voluntary system.

"This current process is working very well and fully protects public health," says McClellan. "To the best of our knowledge, all bioengineered foods on the market have been evaluated by FDA through the current consultation process." This includes genetically engineered foods produced by companies outside the United States and marketed here. . . .

Several private and government organizations have studied the safety of genetically engineered foods. In a study released in 2000, a committee of the National Academy of Sciences (NAS) concluded, "The committee is not aware of any evidence that foods on the market are unsafe to eat as a result of genetic modification." This conclusion was echoed in a report published by the Government Accounting Office in 2002. On the animal side, the international Organization for Economic Cooperation and Development published a consensus document in 2003. It noted that there is no evidence to date from animal feeding studies with bioengineered plants that the performance of animals differed in any respect from those fed the non-bioengineered counterpart. . . .

Future Foods and Regulatory Challenges

The first generation of genetically engineered crops was developed primarily to benefit the growers. Plants were created to resist pests and diseases and to tolerate herbicides used to kill weeds. Scientists see the next generation of genetically engineered products benefiting consumers directly. They are adding nutrients to foods to help prevent diseases, reducing allergens and toxins, and making foods tastier.

Using the tools of biotechnology, researchers are working to reduce the bitterness in citrus fruits, reduce saturated fats in cooking oils, produce more flavorful tomatoes, and even lessen the gassiness caused by beans. Grains, fruits and vegetables that contain more nutrients and potatoes that absorb less oil when made into chips and french fries are also in the development pipeline. . . .

To . . . assure that the FDA has the best scientific knowledge available to assess the safety of genetically engineered foods, the agency has increased the number of staff experts in plant genetics, molecular biology, immunology, and agricultural biotechnology.

In addition to its own scientists who evaluate safety data, the FDA looks to outside experts, such as the NAS, for advice on food safety assessments. In response to public concerns about the unknown long-term effects of consuming genetically engineered foods, the FDA, USDA and EPA requested assistance from the NAS. The NAS is currently conducting a study to assess the potential for unintended health effects resulting from genetically engineered foods.

"We have no reason to believe there are any adverse effects from the long-term use of these foods," says Maryanski, "but we've asked the NAS to look into it as part of our continuing effort to make sure that our decisions are based on the best science available today."

The FDA has added members with agricultural biotech expertise to its advisory committees that address scientific questions related to bioengineered foods and animal feeds. These committees also include consumer representatives.

"The FDA will continue to reach out to the public to help consumers understand the scientific issues and the agency's policies regarding genetically engineered food," says McClellan. "FDA, in cooperation with USDA and EPA, will continue its oversight of new and emerging food biotechnology products and will be vigilant in ensuring the safety and integrity of the food supply.". . .

Reducing Allergens

One concern about genetic engineering is that scientists might unknowingly create or enhance a food allergen. But researchers are hoping that this powerful technology can be used to eliminate or reduce allergens, such as those found in peanuts, wheat and soy.

Experts estimate that 8 percent of children 6 years old and younger and 1 to 2 percent of adults have food allergies, which can cause severe, and sometimes life-threatening, reactions.

Early attempts to eliminate a food allergen have yielded promising results. In 2002, researchers genetically engineered soy to eliminate expression of a common soy protein. Soy allergies are particularly common in infants and young children, according to the National Institute of Allergy and Infectious Diseases. It's difficult to avoid eating soy because of its wide use in many processed foods, including infant formula, cereals, and salad dressings.

Using a "gene silencing" technique, researchers were able to "knock out" a gene that makes a protein called P34, which is thought to trigger most allergic reactions to soy. Tests on blood from people allergic to soy showed no antibody response to the plant with the knocked-out gene, indicating that the allergen could not be detected. The plant's characteristics were also analyzed. "We see no change in the pattern of growth, productivity, or protein composition," says Eliot Herman, Ph.D., lead researcher on this project and molecular biologist at the U.S. Department of Agriculture's Agricultural Research Service.

The work is not done yet, cautions Herman. "There are up to 15 different proteins in soybeans that people are allergic to," he says. "The major one, P34, is responsible for 75 percent of the allergic reactions. How much do you have to get rid of to not trigger an allergic response at all? This is what we need to find out."

Herman sees the benefit of genetically engineered soy in both human food and animal feed. "Baby pigs are similar to baby humans in their reaction to soybeans," he says. "They have gastric distress too." Herman's team is studying the reaction of piglets to the genetically engineered soy, and these studies may pave the way to human clinical trials.

'Pharm' Factories of the Future

Plants may become miniature "factories" for pharmaceuticals through genetic engineering. Scientists are growing plants that produce antibodies to help fight cancer, heart disease and tooth decay. And researchers are experimenting with growing fruits and vegetables that contain vaccines for measles, hepatitis B, Norwalk virus, diarrhea, cholera and more.

These edible vaccines could be pureed into an applesauce-like consistency and fed to children and adults alike. They could be produced in larger quantities and at less expense than current vaccines, although they will have to be grown and handled under strict conditions imposed by the U.S. Department of Agriculture (USDA) aimed at ensuring that they do not inadvertently enter the food supply.

The Food and Drug Administration regulates pharmaceuticals, whether they are manufactured in traditional factories or in crops in the field, to ensure their safety, purity and potency. The FDA and the USDA have jointly published draft guidance specifically addressing the use of bioengineered plants to produce pharmaceutical products.

The FDA is also part of a White House National Economic Council working group that is addressing the regulation of genetically engineered crops to ensure there are no gaps in protecting human health and the environment.

"Mounting evidence . . . suggests that [genetically modified] foods are not safe."

Genetically Engineered Foods Will Harm Americans

Jeffrey M. Smith

In the following viewpoint Jeffrey M. Smith warns that studies purporting to show that genetically engineered (GE) foods are safe are superficial and unreliable. Instead, he argues, there are numerous reliable studies that suggest that GE foods are unsafe for both human and animal consumption. Millions of Americans are being exposed to these potentially hazardous foods without their knowledge, Smith maintains, and may face serious health problems as a result. Smith is director of the Institute for Responsible Technology and author of *Seeds of Deception: Exposing Industry and Government Lies About the Safety of the Genetically Engineered Foods You're Eating.*

As you read, consider the following questions:

1. What was the death rate of chickens fed GE corn, compared to those fed natural corn, according to Smith?
2. As explained by the author, what did the only human feeding study of soybeans show?
3. According to Smith, what has been the consumer response to GE foods in other countries, where the press has been more open about their potential dangers?

In a study in the early 1990's rats were fed genetically modified (GM) tomatoes. Well actually, the rats refused to eat them. They were force-fed. Several of the rats developed stomach lesions and seven out of forty died within two weeks. Scientists at the FDA [Food and Drug Administration] who reviewed the study agreed that it did not provide a "demonstration of reasonable certainty of no harm." In fact, agency scientists warned that GM foods in general might create unpredicted allergies, toxins, antibiotic resistant diseases, and nutritional problems. Internal FDA memos made public from a lawsuit reveal that the scientists urged their superiors to require long-term safety testing to catch these hard-to-detect side effects. But FDA political appointees, including a former attorney for [biotechnology company] Monsanto in charge of policy, ignored the scientists' warnings. The FDA does not require safety studies. Instead, if the makers of the GM foods claim that they are safe, the agency has no further questions. The GM tomato was approved in 1994.

Mounting Evidence of Possible Harm

According to a July 27, 2004, report from the US National Academy of Sciences (NAS), the current system of blanket approval of GM foods by the FDA might not detect "unintended changes in the composition of the food." The process of gene insertion, according to the NAS, could damage the host's DNA with unpredicted consequences. The Indian Council of Medical Research (ICMR), which released its findings a few days earlier, identified a long list of potentially dangerous side effects from GM foods that are not being evaluated. The ICMR called for a complete overhaul of existing regulations.

The safety studies conducted by the biotech industry are often dismissed by critics as superficial and designed to avoid finding problems. Tragically, scientists who voice their criticism, as well as those who have discovered incriminating evidence, have been threatened, stripped of responsibilities, denied funding or tenure, or fired. For example, a UK [United Kingdom] government-funded study demonstrated that rats fed a GM potato developed potentially pre-cancerous cell growth, damaged immune systems, partial atrophy of the liver, and inhibited development of their brains, livers and testicles. When the lead scientist went public with his concerns, he was promptly fired from his job after 35 years and silenced with threats of a lawsuit.

Americans eat genetically modified foods every day. Although the GM tomato has been taken off the market, millions of acres of soy, corn, canola, and cotton have had foreign genes inserted into their DNA. The new genes allow the crops to survive applications of herbicide, create their own pesticide, or both. While there are only a handful of published animal safety studies, mounting evidence, which needs to be followed up, suggests that these foods are not safe.

Rats fed GM corn had problems with blood cell formation. Those fed GM soy had problems with liver cell formation, and the livers of rats fed GM canola were heavier. Pigs fed GM corn on several Midwest farms developed false pregnancies or sterility. Cows fed GM corn in Germany died mysteriously. And twice the number of chickens died when fed GM corn compared to those fed natural corn.

Allergies to GM Food

Soon after GM soy was introduced to the UK, soy allergies skyrocketed by 50 percent. Without follow-up tests, we can't be sure if genetic engineering was the cause, but there are plenty of ways in which genetic manipulation can boost allergies.

- A gene from a Brazil nut inserted into soybeans made the soy allergenic to those who normally react to Brazil nuts.
- GM soy currently consumed in the US contains a gene from bacteria. The inserted gene creates a protein that was never before part of the human food supply, and might be allergenic.
- Sections of that protein are identical to those found in shrimp and dust mite allergens. According to criteria recommended by the World Health Organization (WHO), this fact should have disqualified GM soy from approval.
- The sequence of the gene that was inserted into soy has

inexplicably rearranged over time. The protein it creates is likely to be different than the one intended, and was never subject to any safety studies. It may be allergenic or toxic.

- The process of inserting the foreign gene damaged a section of the soy's own DNA, scrambling its genetic code. This mutation might interfere with DNA expression or create a new, potentially dangerous protein.
- The most common allergen in soy is called trypsin inhibitor. GM soy contains significantly more of this compared with natural soy.

Gene Transfer

The only human feeding study ever conducted showed that the gene inserted into soybeans spontaneously transferred out of food and into the DNA of gut bacteria. This has several serious implications. First, it means that the bacteria inside our intestines, newly equipped with this foreign gene, may create the novel protein inside of us. If it is allergenic or toxic, it may affect us for the long term, even if we give up eating GM soy.

The same study verified that the promoter, which scientists attach to the inserted gene to permanently switch it on, also transferred to gut bacteria. Research on this promoter suggests that it might unintentionally switch on other genes in the DNA—permanently. This could create an overproduction of allergens, toxins, carcinogens, or antinutrients. Scientists also theorize that the promoter might switch on dormant viruses embedded in the DNA or generate mutations.

Unfortunately, gene transfer from GM food might not be limited to our gut bacteria. Preliminary results show that the promoter also transferred into rat organs, after they were fed only a single GM meal.

This is only a partial list of what may go wrong with a single GM food crop. The list for others may be longer. Take for example, the corn inserted with a gene that creates its own pesticide. We eat that pesticide, and plenty of evidence suggests that it is not as benign as the biotech proponents would have us believe. Preliminary evidence, for example, shows that thirty-nine Filipinos living next to a pesticide-producing cornfield developed skin, intestinal, and respiratory reactions while the corn was pollinating. Tests of their blood also showed an immune response to the pesticide. Consider what might happen if the gene that produces the pesticide were to transfer from the corn we eat into our gut bacteria. It could theoretically transform our intestinal flora into living pesticide factories.

P.J. Polyp. © 2001 by *The New Internationalist*. Reproduced by permission.

GM corn and most GM crops are also inserted with antibiotic resistant genes. The ICMR, along with the American Medical Association, the WHO, and organizations worldwide, have expressed concern about the possibility that these might transfer to pathogenic bacteria inside our gut. They are afraid that it might create new, antibiotic resistant super-diseases. The defense that the biotech industry used to counter these fears was that the DNA was fully destroyed during digestion and therefore no such transfer of genes was possible. The human feeding study described above, published in February 2004, overturned this baseless assumption.

A Dangerous Lack of Awareness

No one monitors human health impacts of GM foods. If the foods were creating health problems in the US population, it might take years or decades before we identified the cause. One epidemic in the 1980's provides a chilling example. A new disease was caused by a brand of the food supplement L-tryptophan, which had been created through genetic modification and contained tiny traces of contaminants. The disease killed about 100 Americans and caused sickness or disability in about 5–10,000 others. The only reason that doctors were able to identify that an epidemic was occurring, was because the disease had three simultaneous characteristics: it was rare, acute, and fast acting. Even then it was nearly missed entirely.

Studies show that the more people learn about GM foods, the less they trust them. In Europe, Japan, and other regions, the press has been far more open about the potential dangers of genetic manipulation. Consequently, consumers there demand that their food supply be GM-free and manufacturers comply. But in the US, most people believe they have never eaten a GM food in their lives (even though they consume them daily). Lacking awareness, complacent consumers have been the key asset for the biotech industry in the US. As a result, millions of Americans are exposed to the potential dangers, and children are most at risk. Perhaps the revelations in the reports released on opposite sides of the planet will awaken consumers as well as regulators, and GM foods on the market will be withdrawn.

"Hydrogen solves simultaneously an assortment of problems, from political to environmental to medical."

Hydrogen Will Be the Answer to America's Energy Problems

Julian Gresser and James A. Cusumano

In the following viewpoint Julian Gresser and James A. Cusumano maintain that the United States can, and must, make the transition from fossil fuel dependence to a hydrogen economy. Worldwide oil supplies will soon be depleted, they argue, creating an energy crisis in America. By investing in hydrogen technology, say Gresser and Cusumano, America will have a safe, clean energy source that will drive economic growth and prosperity. Gresser, chairman of Alliances for Discovery, has served as an adviser to the U.S. State Department, the prime minister's office of Japan, and the European Commission. Cusumano is founder of Catalytica Energy Systems, Inc. and a former research director for Exxon.

As you read, consider the following questions:

1. As predicted by British Petroleum, cited by the authors, how many years of oil are left in the ground?
2. How would a hydrogen economy be beneficial to human health, according to the authors?
3. What is the true per-gallon price of gasoline, as argued by Gresser and Cusumano?

S hifting the global economy away from dependence on rapidly depleting supplies of oil to renewable, clean-burning hydrogen must happen sooner rather than later. Any thought that the transition can be gradually implemented over the next 40 to 50 years mistakenly assumes that there will continue to be enough cheap oil for the foreseeable future and that new discoveries and technological innovations can always fill in any gaps. Such assumptions are seriously flawed and imperil national and international stability.

In 1956, Shell Oil geologist M. King Hubbert predicted that U.S. oil production (barrels pumped per year) would peak in the early 1970s. Most geologists at the time rejected Hubbert's analysis until 1970 when oil production peaked within the lower 48 states. Since then, numerous respected geologists have refined Hubbert's methodology and have applied it to worldwide oil production, country by country. They concluded that world production of oil will peak between 2004 and 2008. Today [2005], as in 1956, many industry and most political leaders either reject this analysis or ignore its projected consequences.

Most geologists estimate that about 2 trillion barrels of oil were formed in the earth over millions of years. To date we have pumped out about half of this supply. Despite years of generous government subsidies and continuing worldwide investments by the global oil industry to accelerate technological innovation, the rate of discovery of new oil sources began declining decades ago and has never recovered. British Petroleum (BP) reports that proven oil reserves increased from 0.7 trillion barrels in 1981 to 1 trillion barrels in 1991 to only 1.03 trillion barrels in 2001. BP, as do most oil companies, uses the R/P method to measure how much oil is left worldwide. It divides known reserves (R in barrels) by the production rate (P in barrels per year) and this gives the "years of oil left in the ground." Using this method, BP predicts 40 years of oil left in the ground.

The problem with this approach is it implies things will be fine until we pump the last drop of oil out of the ground 40 years from now. But things won't be free, according to Hubbert's analysis. Economic dislocations will begin to occur exponentially once we reach the halfway point (the peak) in consuming the oil in the ground. A policy of relying on things to be fine seems dangerously naive. . . .

The wisest way to anticipate and mitigate this risk would be to implement an immediate "quantum jump" into energy conservation and hydrogen development. . . . To be sure, even this quantum jump strategy will likely require 15 to 20 years to achieve broad displacement of current oil sources by hydrogen.

The U.S. Energy, Commerce, and Defense departments already have in place programs to promote hydrogen. These programs . . . are not nearly comprehensive or timely enough to meet the challenges before us.

What is required is a program on the scale of the Manhattan Project or NASA [National Aeronautics and Space Administration]'s Apollo Program,[1] with two essential elements: (1) massive and immediate energy conservation to reduce oil dependence, and (2) an international, entrepreneurial, multipronged initiative to accelerate global economic growth and prosperity based on hydrogen.

Energy Conservation and Oil Independence

Among the immediate steps that could be taken to reduce U.S. dependence on foreign oil by a significant amount are:

- Commercial and residential buildings must be retrofitted with known state-of-the-art, energy-efficient systems for lighting, appliances, and heating/air-conditioning systems.
- Oil usage in transportation—for cars, trucks, buses, trains, and even aircraft—should be substantially reduced within three to five years.
- Tax breaks and other incentives must be made available to consumers who purchase energy-efficient vehicles such as gas-electric hybrid cars.
- Public utilities must be required by law, as in Japan, to deliver a meaningful percentage of electricity derived from sustainable energy sources.

1. The Manhattan Project was an effort by the United States during World War II to develop the first nuclear weapons. It culminated in the detonation of three nuclear weapons in 1945. The Apollo Project was devoted to landing a man on the moon, which was achieved in 1969.

To be sure, the biggest impact will come from cutting back on the 13 million barrels per day (out of a total of 20 million barrels per day) of oil that drives the U.S. transportation system.

The benefits will be immediate and massive, including reduced vulnerability to terrorist attacks against oil storage and transportation lines in the Persian Gulf and elsewhere. And thousands of new jobs would be created as workers flock to new opportunities in the Hydrogen Economy.

Internationally, there are precedents for such a massive, "Apollo" level undertaking. During the 1980s, China's efficiency program reduced overall energy usage within a decade by 50%, while China's economic growth led, and continues to lead, the developing world. In the 1980s, Denmark began a crash program in wind-generated electricity. Today, wind provides 10% of Denmark's power while that country makes 60% of all the wind turbines sold in the world. India's Renewable Energy Development Agency launched a similar set of initiatives beginning in 1987, and today India is the world's largest user of photovoltaic systems for generating distributive electrical energy.

The United States has also succeeded in the past in energy conservation. Corporate Average Fuel Economy (CAFE) standards more than doubled the average mileage of U.S. automobiles between 1975 and 1985. Efficiency programs sponsored by the Department of Energy returned $20 for every $1 invested, making them one of the best investments in the economy even before a change in national energy strategy, according to economics writer Robert Freeman. The Worldwatch Institute reports that energy efficiency measures enacted since 1975 saved the United States an estimated $365 billion in 2000 alone.

Crucial Questions for the Hydrogen Alternative

Immediate energy conservation must be tightly coupled to a coherent plan to expedite the transition to a viable, global alternative—hydrogen. Four questions are crucial: Why hydrogen? Is hydrogen a timely and viable option? Is hydrogen safe? Can hydrogen become an engine for global growth and prosperity?

Why Hydrogen?

Hydrogen solves simultaneously an assortment of problems, from political to environmental to medical. In addition to reducing global dependence on Middle Eastern oil and the oil infrastructure's vulnerability to terrorist attacks, a Hydrogen Economy would democratize energy generation so that all nations can have equal access to the benefits of electricity. It would reduce emissions of carbon dioxide and toxic air contaminants, since hydrogen generated by wind or solar power results solely in water as a by-product. It would reduce diseases such as asthma, emphysema, and asthmatic bronchitis, which are closely associated with air pollution from fossil fuels. And the Hydrogen Economy would mitigate, and in time possibly prevent, disruptive climatic changes, including global warming, which are now widely recognized as caused by sharply rising carbon dioxide concentrations in the atmosphere.

Is Hydrogen a Timely and Viable Option?

Present U.S. industrial policies favoring a petroleum-based economy have cost the American people $3.4 trillion over the last 30 years, according to a study by the Institute for the Analysis of Global Security. Oil imports account for one-third of the total U.S. deficit and therefore are a major source of unemployment. The true social costs of a fossil fuel-based economy should also include the billions upon billions of dollars of damage to health, property, and the environment.

Thus, hydrogen's economic viability needs to be examined in the context of the current, distorted, subsidized price for oil. For example, if the petroleum industry were required today to bear the full costs of its health, property, and environmental damages, the present price of gasoline at the pump would easily rise to more than $15 per gallon, and the price of electricity would increase from 3 cents per kilowatt-hour to more than 30 cents, according to Peter Hoffmann, author of *Tomorrow's Energy*. Additionally, this price would rise substantially higher if it accurately reflected numerous other hidden costs—for example, more than $50 billion per year even before the 2003 Iraq war in military personnel and equipment required to protect U.S. oil interests in the Middle East. The current price of $2.50–$5 per gallon-equivalent of ultra-clean hydrogen, produced by solar or wind-powered electrolysis, would be immediately competitive.

Safety Benefits of Hydrogen

Hydrogen is no more or less dangerous than other flammable fuels, including gasoline and natural gas. In fact, some of hydrogen's differences actually provide safety benefits compared to gasoline or other fuels. . . .

Hydrogen has a rapid diffusivity (3.8 times faster than natural gas), which means that when released, it dilutes quickly into a non-flammable concentration. Hydrogen rises 2 times faster than helium and 6 times faster than natural gas at a speed of almost 45 mph (20m/s).Therefore, unless a roof, a poorly ventilated room or some other structure contains the rising gas, the laws of physics prevent hydrogen from lingering near a leak (or near people using hydrogen-fueled equipment). . . .

Like any flammable fuel, hydrogen can combust. But hydrogen's buoyancy, diffusivity and small molecular size make it difficult to contain and create a combustible situation. . . .

Hydrogen is non-toxic and non-poisonous. It will not contaminate groundwater (it's a gas under normal atmospheric conditions), nor will a release of hydrogen contribute to atmospheric pollution. Hydrogen does not create "fumes."

National Hydrogen Association, www.hydrogenassociates.org, 2005.

Hydrogen technologies are remarkably robust and near to becoming economically viable today. Hydrogen is already a highly desirable alternative when we consider the economics of the entire system. For example, the present wellhead-to-wheels efficiency of the gasoline internal combustion engine is 14%—i.e., 14% of the energy extracted from oil in the ground ends up powering your car. If we use natural gas as the interim source of hydrogen until solar/wind electrolyzers are more available with higher efficiencies, the current wellhead-to-wheels efficiency of a hydrogen fuel-cell car is 42%, or three times greater. The comparative efficiencies of hydrogen over gasoline are also apparent in cars with hydrogen internal combustion engines, which could provide a short-term transition strategy.

Hydrogen generation, storage, and distribution could also take place locally, thereby deconcentrating vulnerable power supplies and strongly encouraging local energy independence, self-reliance, and innovation. Hydrogen pipeline investments should be deferred to the future when the Hydrogen Economy is well under way, and this investment makes economic sense.

If, as we propose, oil production will peak within this decade, the Hydrogen Economy is our only short-term and long-term option. The basics of hydrogen science have been known for many years, and technological breakthroughs can be further accelerated and optimized by sharply focused industry and government research programs. Coal and nuclear fission have significant environmental challenges, and nuclear fusion will not likely be viable until the latter part of this century.

Is Hydrogen Safe?

Hydrogen is sometimes associated with the Hindenburg disaster,[2] which occurred at Lakehurst, New Jersey, in 1937. However, a detailed analysis by former NASA scientist Addison Bain found that this incident would have occurred in much the same manner even if the dirigible had been filled with nonflammable helium gas.

The fire started in the diesel engine room and quickly spread to the dirigible's outer coating, which was a highly flammable material similar to that used in rocket propellants. It is unlikely that anyone was killed by a hydrogen fire. (There was no explosion.) One-third of the passengers died by jumping from the cabin; the others survived by riding the dirigible to the ground as the ultralight, rapidly diffusing hydrogen gas burned harmlessly above them.

For the same given volume, the explosive power of gasoline is 22 times more potent than that for hydrogen gas. Furthermore, the global hydrogen industry has an impeccable safety record.

---

2. In 1937 this German zeppelin filled with hydrogen caught fire and burned while airborne, killing thirty-five passengers and one member of the ground crew.

Hydrogen as an Engine for Global Economic Growth and Prosperity

Perhaps the greatest political appeal and the most immediate beneficial impact of the Hydrogen Economy is the emergence of hydrogen as a strategic business sector and an engine of global economic growth within the decade and for the remainder of the twenty-first century.

Throughout history, certain industries experiencing breakthroughs in technology have served as engines of economic growth. Economic growth occurs when gains in productivity in the strategic business sector are rapidly transferred through innovation and the convergence of the key technologies to other industries and sectors. Among the most famous examples are the canals and railroads in the eighteenth and nineteenth centuries in Europe and the United States, machine tool making in New England in the early nineteenth century, and the German chemical dye industry in the late nineteenth century. Japan's post–World War II industries— steel, autos, household electronics, semiconductors, computers, telecommunications, and robotics—illustrate how economic leverage can multiply when innovations in one strategic sector trigger breakthroughs in the next.

Because the public benefits of strategic technologies and industries are significant, as are the commercial risks, governments have usually played a critical role, especially during the early stages, in nurturing and accelerating their development. For example, rural electrification in the United States would have taken generations without strong government support during Franklin Roosevelt's administration. Today, the state of California has taken the lead in implementing the Hydrogen Highway Network Action Plan, and will build 150–200 hydrogen fueling stations throughout the state, approximately one every 20 miles on California's major highways. California's Hydrogen Highway is an "economically strategic instrumentality," which, like the railroads in the nineteenth century, will drive economic growth in a wide spectrum of user industries.

Florida has also launched an imaginative program to promote hydrogen as a strategic sector. Florida's Hydrogen Strategy is based on alliances among private companies, state and local government organizations, universities, environmental groups, and select groups from the space program. Initial areas of focus are fuel cells, internal combustion engines retrofitted to run on hydrogen, hydrogen storage, and power-grid optimization. Financial incentives include tax refunds, investment tax credits, performance incentives, quick response training programs, and enterprise bond financing.

Japan, Germany, Canada, and Iceland all understand that hydrogen's development is economically strategic, as it will drive innovations in nanomaterials, biotechnology, solar photocatalysis, and even the Internet through local, distributed generation. These countries are vigorously supporting their transition away from oil.

An Apollo Mission for Hydrogen

The United States needs to build rapid political consensus for a Hydrogen Economy. To start, the U.S. government should assemble a task force that includes the nation's leading hydrogen scientists and technologists, inventors, environmental and natural resource lawyers, experts on public finance, and specialists on public/private alliances. Their assignment should be to produce within six months a draft "Strategic Hydrogen Alliance Reform and Enterprise Act" (SHARE), which will reward manufacturers, motivate customers, and amplify support for basic and applied research. Public/private alliances can be the engine to gather the nation's entrepreneurial energies behind hydrogen.

As hydrogen becomes a strategic economic driver for the United States and the major industrialized nations, it can serve this same function for many other countries, rich and poor. The size and commercial risks of some hydrogen projects make them ideal candidates for international collaboration. As new countries enter the hydrogen consortium, each can develop special domains of leverage and comparative advantage based on its unique skills and resources. An international initiative for hydrogen is needed that emulates the vigor, imagination, and support of humanity's most visionary endeavors, such as the Human Genome Project [to map the human genome] or [former] President [John F.] Kennedy's

Apollo Project, the vision to land a man on the Moon.

Alliances can act as powerful drivers of innovation. The international initiative should strongly encourage such public/private hydrogen alliances with a focus on special domains of leverage—for example, accelerating cost breakthroughs in hydrogen storage, or generation by wind and solar power—where an investment of time, effort, capital, and creativity could produce scientific and technological breakthroughs with huge commercial and public returns.

The cornerstone of the program and its financial engine is the International Hydrogen Innovation Fund (IHIF), which could be capitalized with investments from national and international governments, corporations, and nonprofit foundations. It should be managed by an international team of experienced business and social entrepreneurs with demonstrated records of success. The IHIF would aim to achieve a superior rate of return within five years for its shareholders (including governments and other public entities), based on its investments in early, middle, and late stage projects.

If imaginatively conceived and effectively implemented, this international hydrogen initiative can be financially self-sustaining from the outset. Moreover, the IHIF's asset portfolio can be further strengthened as the IHIF negotiates rights in patents and other properties of the public/private alliances it spawns and supports. This strategy in itself will constitute a significant innovation for many government leaders who today ardently wish to support worthy public ventures but lack the financial means to do so.

Entering the Hydrogen Age

A curtain is rising on the next act in the human story. We are each protagonists and playwrights in this drama. The likely scene is a tragedy: intense competition and conflict over rapidly depleting oil reserves; devastation of remaining ecologically fragile, oil-rich areas; panicked decisions to shift to coal or nuclear options that will further pollute the earth and destroy its beauty; and grinding poverty, despair, and hopelessness for most of humanity.

There is another, brighter scenario. It is based on hydrogen, when clean and self-sustaining energy replaces established, exploitative technologies, and citizens everywhere use their unique talents to fashion the world anew. The transition will not be easy, but a few courageous and farsighted leaders working with the international community can take the tide at its flood and begin to lead the world to a better fortune.

"Waiting for hydrogen to save us isn't an option."

Hydrogen Will Not Be the Answer to America's Energy Problems

Michael Behar

While hydrogen may be a useful source of energy in the future, says Michael Behar in the following viewpoint, currently there are numerous and significant technological and financial obstacles to its immediate use. Hydrogen power is still difficult to produce and use, he maintains, and it will not provide the clean, abundant power that America needs any time in the near future. Behar is a freelance writer based in Washington, D.C. He has contributed to *Wired*, *Outside*, *Smithsonian*, and *Discover* magazines.

As you read, consider the following questions:

1. What might be the impact of increased hydrogen in the atmosphere, according to Behar?
2. As argued by the author, why is it easier for Iceland to utilize hydrogen power than it is for the United States?
3. Why would hydrogen-powered cars need huge fuel tanks, as explained by Behar?

In the presidential campaign of 2004, [George W.] Bush and [John] Kerry managed to find one piece of common ground: Both spoke glowingly of a future powered by fuel cells. Hydrogen would free us from our dependence on fossil fuels and would dramatically curb emissions of air pollutants, including carbon dioxide, the gas chiefly blamed for global warming. The entire worldwide energy market would evolve into a "hydrogen economy" based on clean, abundant power. Auto manufacturers and environmentalists alike happily rode the bandwagon, pointing to hydrogen as the next big thing in U.S. energy policy. Yet the truth is that we aren't much closer to a commercially viable hydrogen-powered car than we are to cold fusion or a cure for cancer. This hardly surprises engineers, fuel cell manufacturers and policymakers, who have known all along that the technology has been hyped, perhaps to its detriment, and that the public has been misled about what Howard Coffman, editor of fuelcellinfo.com, describes as the "undeniable realities of the hydrogen economy." These experts are confident that the hydrogen economy will arrive—someday. But first, they say, we have to overcome daunting technological, financial and political roadblocks. Herewith, our checklist of misconceptions and doubts about hydrogen and the exalted fuel cell.

1. Hydrogen Is an Abundant Fuel

True, hydrogen is the most common element in the universe; it's so plentiful that the sun consumes 600 million tons of it every second. But unlike oil, vast reservoirs of hydrogen don't exist here on Earth. Instead, hydrogen atoms are bound up in molecules with other elements, and we must expend energy to extract the hydrogen so it can be used in fuel cells. We'll never get more energy out of hydrogen than we put into it.

"Hydrogen is a currency, not a primary energy source," explains Geoffrey Ballard, the father of the modern-day fuel cell and co-founder of Ballard Power Systems, the world's leading fuel-cell developer. "It's a means of getting energy from where you created it to where you need it."

2. Hydrogen Fuel Cells Will End Global Warming

Unlike internal combustion engines, hydrogen fuel cells do not emit carbon dioxide [CO_2]. But extracting hydrogen from natural gas, today's primary source, does. And wresting hydrogen from water through electrolysis takes tremendous amounts of energy. If that energy comes from power plants burning fossil fuels, the end product may be clean hydrogen, but the process used to obtain it is still dirty.

Once hydrogen is extracted, it must be compressed and transported, presumably by machinery and vehicles that in the early stages of a hydrogen economy will be running on fossil fuels. The result: even more CO_2. In fact, driving a fuel cell car with hydrogen extracted from natural gas or water could produce a net increase of CO_2 in the atmosphere. "People say that hydrogen cars would be pollution-free," observes University of Calgary engineering professor David Keith. "Lightbulbs are pollution-free, but power plants are not."

In the short term, nuclear power may be the easiest way to produce hydrogen without pumping more carbon dioxide into the atmosphere. Electricity from a nuclear plant would electrolyze water—splitting H_2O into hydrogen and oxygen. Ballard champions the idea, calling nuclear power "extremely important, unless we see some other major breakthrough that none of us has envisioned."

Critics counter that nuclear power creates long-term waste problems and isn't economically competitive. An exhaustive industry analysis entitled "The Future of Nuclear Power," written last year [2004] by 10 professors from the Massachusetts Institute of Technology and Harvard University, concludes that "hydrogen produced by electrolysis of water depends on low-cost nuclear power." As long as electricity from nuclear power costs more than electricity from other sources, using that energy to make hydrogen doesn't add up.

3. The Hydrogen Economy Can Run on Renewable Energy

Perform electrolysis with renewable energy, such as solar or wind power, and you eliminate the pollution issues associated with fossil fuels and nuclear power. Trouble is, renewable sources can provide only a small fraction of the energy that will be required for a full-fledged hydrogen economy.

From 1998 to 2003, the generating capacity of wind power increased 28 percent in the U.S. to 6,374 megawatts, enough for roughly 1.6 million homes. The wind industry expects to meet 6 percent of the country's electricity needs by 2020. But economist Andrew Oswald of the University of Warwick in England calculates that converting every vehicle in the U.S. to hydrogen power would require the electricity output of a million wind turbines—enough to cover half of California. Solar panels would likewise require huge swaths of land.

Water is another limiting factor for hydrogen production, especially in the sunny regions most suitable for solar power. According to a study done by the World Resources Institute, a Washington, D.C.–based nonprofit organization, fueling a hydrogen economy with electrolysis would require 4.2 trillion gallons of water annually—roughly the amount that flows over Niagara Falls every three months. Overall, U.S. water consumption would increase by about 10 percent.

4. Hydrogen Gas Leaks Are Nothing to Worry About

Hydrogen gas is odorless and colorless, and it burns almost invisibly. A tiny fire may go undetected at a leaky fuel pump until your pant leg goes up in flames. And it doesn't take much to set compressed hydrogen gas alight. "A cellphone or a lightning storm puts out enough static discharge to ignite hydrogen," claims Joseph Romm, author of *The Hype about Hydrogen: Fact and Fiction in the Race to Save the Climate* and founder of the Center for Energy and Climate Solutions in Arlington, Virginia.

A fender bender is unlikely to spark an explosion, because carbon-fiber-reinforced hydrogen tanks are virtually indestructible. But that doesn't eliminate the danger of leaks elsewhere in what will eventually be a huge network of refineries, pipelines and fueling stations. "The obvious pitfall is that hydrogen is a gas, and most of our existing petrochemical sources are liquids," says Robert Uhrig, professor emeritus of nuclear engineering at the University of Tennessee and former vice president of Florida Power & Light. "The infrastructure required to support high-pressure gas or cryogenic liquid hydrogen is much more complicated. Hydrogen is one of those things that people have great difficulty confining. It tends to go through the finest of holes."

To calculate the effects a leaky infrastructure might have on our atmosphere, a team of researchers from the California Institute of Technology and the Jet Propulsion Laboratory in Pasadena, California, looked at statistics for accidental industrial hydrogen and natural gas leakage—estimated at 10 to 20 percent of total volume—and then predicted how much leakage might occur in an economy in which everything runs on hydrogen. Result: The amount of hydrogen in the atmosphere would be four to eight times as high as it is today.

Not the Best Solution

Setting up a completely new infrastructure to distribute hydrogen would cost at least $5,000 per vehicle. Transporting, storing and distributing a gaseous fuel as opposed to a liquid raises many new problems.

More billions of dollars will be needed to develop hydrogen fuel cells that can match the performance of today's gasoline engines. . . .

The benefits might be worth the costs of fuel-cell development and creating a new infrastructure, however, if air pollution, greenhouse gases and imported petroleum could not be reduced in other ways. But they can. . . .

Improvements to current cars and current environmental rules are more than 100 times cheaper than hydrogen cars at reducing air pollution. And for several decades, the most cost-effective method to reduce oil imports and CO_2 emissions from cars will be to increase fuel efficiency.

Robert Sanders, *UC Berkeley News*, July 17, 2003.

The Caltech study "grossly overstated" hydrogen leakage, says Assistant Secretary David Garman of the Department of Energy's Office of Energy Efficiency and Renewable Energy. But whatever its volume, hydrogen added to the atmosphere will combine with oxygen to form water vapor, creating noctilucent clouds—those high, wispy tendrils you see at dawn and dusk. The increased cloud cover could accelerate global warming.

5. Cars Are the Natural First Application for Hydrogen Fuel Cells

"An economically sane, cost-effective attack on the climate problem wouldn't start with cars," David Keith says. Cars and light trucks contribute roughly 20 percent of the carbon dioxide emitted in the U.S., while power plants burning fossil fuels are responsible for more than 40 percent of CO_2 emissions. Fuel cells designed for vehicles must cope with harsh conditions and severe limitations on size and weight.

A better solution to global warming might be to hold off building hydrogen cars, and instead harness fuel cells to generate electricity for homes and businesses. Plug Power, UTC, FuelCell Energy and Ballard Power Systems already market stationary fuel-cell generators. Plug Power alone has 161 systems in the U.S., including the first fuel-cell-powered McDonald's. Collectively, however, the four companies have a peak generating capacity of about 69 megawatts, less than 0.01 percent of the total 944,000 megawatts of U.S. generating capacity.

6. The U.S. Is Committed to Hydrogen, Pouring Billions into Research and Development

Consider this: President George W. Bush promised to spend $1.2 billion on hydrogen. Yet he allotted $1.5 billion to promote "healthy marriages." The monthly tab for the war in Iraq is $3.9 billion—a total of $121 billion through last September [2004]. In 2004 the Department of Energy spent more on nuclear and fossil fuel research than on hydrogen.

The federal government's Freedom CAR program, which funds hydrogen R&D [research and development] in conjunction with the big three American carmakers, requires that the companies demonstrate a hydrogen-powered car by 2008—but not that they sell one.

"If you are serious about [hydrogen], you have to commit a whole lot more money," contends Guenter Conzelmann, deputy director of the Center for Energy, Environmental and Economic Systems Analysis at Argonne National Laboratory near Chicago. Conzelmann develops computer models to help the energy industry make predictions about the cost of implementing new technology. His estimate for building a hydrogen economy: more than $500 billion, and that's if 60 percent of Americans continue to drive cars with internal combustion engines.

Shell, ExxonMobil and other oil companies are unwilling

to invest in production, distribution, fueling facilities and storage if there are just a handful of hydrogen cars on the road. Nor will automakers foot the bill and churn out thousands of hydrogen cars if drivers have nowhere to fill them up. Peter Devlin, head of the Department of Energy's hydrogen-production research group, says, "Our industry partners have told us that unless a fourth to a third of all refueling stations in the U.S. offer hydrogen, they won't be willing to take a chance on fuel cells."

To create hydrogen fueling stations, California governor Arnold Schwarzenegger, who drives a Hummer [a large sports utility vehicle], has championed the Hydrogen Highway Project. His plan is to erect 150 to 200 stations—at a cost of at least $500,000 each—along the state's major highways by the end of the decade. So that's one state. Now what about the other 100,775 filling stations in the rest of the U.S.? Retrofitting just 25 percent of those with hydrogen fueling systems would cost more than $13 billion.

7. If Iceland Can Do It, So Can We

Iceland's first hydrogen fueling station is already operating on the outskirts of Reykjavik. The hydrogen, which powers a small fleet of fuel cell buses, is produced onsite from electrolyzed tap water. Meanwhile the recently formed Icelandic New Energy—a consortium that includes automakers, Royal Dutch/Shell and the Icelandic power company Norsk Hydro—is planning to convert the rest of the island nation to a hydrogen system.

Impressive, yes. But 72 percent of Iceland's electricity comes from geothermal and hydroelectric power. With so much readily available clean energy, Iceland can electrolyze water with electricity directly from the national power grid. This type of setup is impossible in the U.S., where only about 15 percent of grid electricity comes from geothermal and hydroelectric sources, while 71 percent is generated by burning fossil fuels.

Another issue is the sheer scale of the system. It could take as few as 16 hydrogen fueling stations to enable Icelanders to drive fuel cell cars anywhere in the country. At close to 90 times the size of Iceland, the U.S. would require a minimum of 1,440 fueling stations. This assumes that stations would be strategically placed to collectively cover the entire U.S. with no overlap and that everyone knows where to find the pumps.

8. Mass Production Will Make Hydrogen Cars Affordable

Simply mass-producing fuel cell cars won't necessarily slash costs. According to Patrick Davis, the former leader of the Department of Energy's fuel cell research team, "If you project today's fuel cell technologies into high-volume production—about 500,000 vehicles a year—the cost is still up to six times too high."

Raj Choudhury, operations manager for the General Motors fuel cell program, claims that GM will have a commercial fuel cell vehicle ready by 2010. Others are doubtful. Ballard says that first there needs to be a "fundamental engineering rethink" of the proton exchange membrane (PEM) fuel cell, the type being developed for automobiles, which still cannot compete with the industry standard for internal combustion engines—a life span of 15 years, or about 170,000 driving miles. Because of membrane deterioration, today's PEM fuel cells typically fail during their first 2,000 hours of operation.

Ballard insists that his original PEM design was merely a prototype. "Ten years ago I said it was the height of engineering arrogance to think that the architecture and geometry we chose to demonstrate the fuel cell in automobiles would be the best architecture and geometry for a commercial automobile," he remarks. "Very few people paid attention to that statement. The truth is that the present geometry isn't getting the price down to where it is commercial. It isn't even entering into the envelope that will allow economies of scale to drive the price down."

In the short term, conventional gasoline-burning vehicles will be replaced by gas-electric hybrids, or by vehicles that burn clean diesel, natural gas, methanol or ethanol. Only later will hydrogen cars make sense, economically and environmentally. "Most analysts think it will take several decades for hydrogen to make a large impact, assuming hydrogen technologies reach their goals," notes Joan Ogden, an associate professor of environmental science and policy at the

University of California at Davis and one of the world's leading researchers of hydrogen energy.

9. Fuel Cell Cars Can Drive Hundreds of Miles on a Single Tank of Hydrogen

A gallon of gasoline contains about 2,600 times the energy of a gallon of hydrogen. If engineers want hydrogen cars to travel at least 300 miles between fill-ups—the automotive-industry benchmark—they'll have to compress hydrogen gas to extremely high pressures: up to 10,000 pounds per square inch.

Even at that pressure, cars would need huge fuel tanks. "High-pressure hydrogen would take up four times the volume of gasoline," says JoAnn Milliken, chief engineer of the Department of Energy's Office of Hydrogen, Fuel Cells and Infrastructure Technologies.

Liquid hydrogen works a bit better. GM's liquid-fueled HydroGen3 goes 250 miles on a tank roughly double the size of that in a standard sedan. But the car must be driven every day to keep the liquid hydrogen chilled to -253 degrees Celsius—just 20 degrees above absolute zero and well below the surface temperature of Pluto—or it boils off. "If your car sits at the airport for a week, you'll have an empty tank when you get back," Milliken says.

If Not Hydrogen, Then What?

The near-future prospects for a hydrogen economy are dim, concludes *The Hydrogen Economy: Opportunities, Costs, Barriers, and R&D Needs*, a major government-sponsored study published last February [2004] by the National Research Council. Representatives from ExxonMobil, Ford, DuPont, the Natural Resources Defense Council and other stakeholders contributed to the report, which urges lawmakers to legislate tougher tailpipe-emission standards and to earmark additional R&D funding for renewable energy and alternative fuels. It foresees "major hurdles on the path to achieving the vision of the hydrogen economy" and recommends that the Department of Energy "keep a balanced portfolio of R&D efforts and continue to explore supply-and demand alternatives that do not depend on hydrogen."

Of course, for each instance where the study points out how hydrogen falls short, there are scores of advocates armed with data to show how it can succeed. Physicist Amory Lovins, who heads the Rocky Mountain Institute, a think tank in Colorado, fastidiously rebuts the most common critiques of hydrogen with an armada of facts and figures in his widely circulated white paper "Twenty Hydrogen Myths." But although he's a booster of hydrogen, Lovins is notably pragmatic. "A lot of silly things have been written both for and against hydrogen," he says. "Some sense of reality is lacking on both sides." He believes that whether the hydrogen economy arrives at the end of this decade or closer to midcentury, interim technologies will play a signal role in the transition.

The most promising of these technologies is the gas-electric hybrid vehicle, which uses both an internal combustion engine and an electric motor, switching seamlessly between the two to optimize gas mileage and engine efficiency. U.S. sales of hybrid cars have been growing steadily, and the 2005 model year saw the arrival of the first hybrid SUVs—the Ford Escape, Toyota Highlander and Lexus RX400h.

Researchers sponsored by the FreedomCAR program are also investigating ultralight materials—plastics, fiberglass, titanium, magnesium, carbon fiber—and developing lighter engines made from aluminum and ceramic materials. These new materials could help reduce vehicle power demands, bridging the cost gap between fossil fuels and fuel cells.

Most experts agree that there is no silver bullet. Instead the key is developing a portfolio of energy-efficient technologies that can help liberate us from fossil fuels and ease global warming. "If we had a wider and more diverse set of energy sources, we'd be more robust, more stable," says Jonathan Pershing, director of the Climate, Energy and Pollution Program at the World Resources Institute. "The more legs your chair rests on, the less likely it is to tip over."

Waiting for hydrogen to save us isn't an option. "If we fail to act during this decade to reduce greenhouse gas emissions, historians will condemn us," Romm writes in *The Hype About Hydrogen*. "And they will most likely be living in a world with a much hotter and harsher climate than ours, one that has undergone an irreversible change for the worse."

5

"If, over the next decade, we convert the U.S. automobile fleet to hybrids . . . we could cut our gasoline use in half."

Gas-Electric Hybrid Automobiles Will Help Reduce U.S. Oil Use

Lester R. Brown

In the following viewpoint Lester R. Brown asserts that by using gas-electric hybrid engines, the United States could significantly reduce its oil consumption. Hybrid engines are extremely energy-efficient, claims Brown. In addition to hybrids he proposes using wind turbines to provide the electricity for these engines, and for other electricity needs across the United States. Not only is wind energy cheap, abundant, and inexhaustible, Brown argues, but it will bring valuable revenue to rural farming communities. Brown is ecology editor for *USA Today Magazine*, president of the Earth Policy Institute, and author of *Plan B: Rescuing a Planet Under Stress and a Civilization in Trouble.*

As you read, consider the following questions:
1. According to the author, how many miles per gallon does the Toyota Prius get in combined highway/city driving?
2. If hybrids received their electricity from wind turbines, what would be the total reduction in U.S. gasoline use, in Brown's estimation?
3. How do yearly royalties from wind turbines compare to the profits of corn or beef produced on the same land, according to the author?

Lester R. Brown, "A Path to Oil Independence," *USA Today Magazine*, vol. 133, January 2005, p. 55. Copyright © 2005 by the Society for the Advancement of Education. Reproduced by permission.

With the price of oil soaring to record levels, political instability in the Middle East on the rise, and little slack in the world oil economy, we need a new energy strategy. Two emerging technologies—gas-electric hybrid engines and advanced-design wind turbines—offer a way to wean the U.S. off of imported oil. If, over the next decade, we convert the U.S. automobile fleet to hybrids with the efficiency of today's Toyota Prius, we could cut our gasoline use in half—no reduction in the number of vehicles or miles driven; just doing it more efficiently.

Hybrids Will Reduce Gasoline Use

At present [2005], three gas-electric models are on the market: the Toyota Prius, Honda Insight, and a hybrid version of the Honda Civic. The midsize Prius—a car on the cutting-edge of automotive technology—gets an astounding 55 mpg [miles per gallon] in combined city/highway driving. No wonder there are lists of eager buyers willing to wait six months for delivery.

Ford recently released a hybrid model of its Escape SUV [sport utility vehicle]. Honda is about to do the same with its popular Accord sedan. General Motors will offer hybrid versions of several of its cars beginning with the Saturn VUE in 2006, followed by the Chevy Tahoe and Malibu. Beyond this, GM has delivered 235 hybrid buses to Seattle, Wash., with the potential to reduce gasoline use there by up to 60%. Other cities slated to go this route are Philadelphia, Pa.; Houston, Tex.; and Portland, Ore.

Wind Power for Hybrids

With hybrid cars now on the market, the stage is set for the second step to reduce oil dependence, the use of wind-generated electricity to power automobiles. If we add to the gas-electric auto a plug-in option and a second battery to increase electricity storage capacity, motorists could do their commuting, shopping, and other short-distance travel largely with electricity, saving gasoline for the occasional long trip. This could lop another 20% off gasoline use in addition to the initial 50% cut from shifting to hybrids, for a total reduction in gasoline use of 70%.

This plug-in ability would give drivers access to the country's vast—and largely untapped—wind resources. In 1991, the Department of Energy published a "National Wind Resource Inventory" in which it pointed out that three states— Kansas, North Dakota, and Texas—have enough harnessable wind energy to satisfy national electricity needs. Many were astonished, since wind power had been considered a marginal energy source. They would be even more amazed today, since the DOE [Department of Energy]'s projections were a gross understatement—as they were based on the wind turbine technologies of 1991.

An Inexhaustible Resource

The average turbine in 1991 was roughly 120 feet tall, whereas new ones are 300 feet high, the equivalent of a 30-story building. Not only does this more than double the harvestable wind regime, but winds at higher elevations are stronger and more reliable.

In Europe, which has emerged as the world leader in developing this type of energy, wind farms satisfy the residential electricity needs of 40,000,000 consumers. In 2003, the European Wind Energy Association projected that, by 2020, wind power would provide electricity for 195,000,000 people—half the population of Western Europe.

Wind power is growing fast because it is cheap, abundant, inexhaustible, widely distributed, clean, and climate-benign. No other energy source has all of these attributes. Moreover, the cost of wind-generated electricity has been in free-fall over the last two decades. The early wind farms in California, where the modern wind industry was born in the early 1980s, generated electricity at a cost of 38 cents per kilowatt-hour. Today, many wind farms are producing power at four cents per kilowatt-hour.

Unlike the widely discussed fuel cell/hydrogen transportation model, the gas-electric hybrid/wind model does not require a costly new infrastructure. The network of gasoline service stations already is in place. So, too, is the electricity grid needed to link wind farms to the storage batteries in cars. Yet, for this new model to work most efficiently, a strong integrated national grid is necessary. The need for modernizing the country's antiquated set of regional grids is widely recognized, especially in light of the

Catalyst for Change?

Rising gas prices are contributing to calls for a change in energy policy that would reduce dependence on foreign oil.

Average price of a gallon of regular gasoline
(adjusted for inflation)

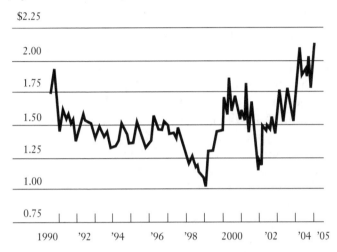

Oil imports as a percent of total oil consumption

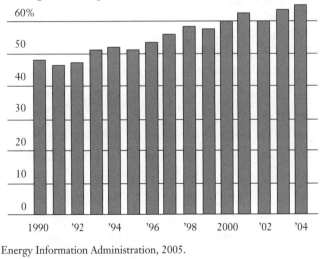

Energy Information Administration, 2005.

blackout that darkened (no pun intended) most of the Northeast in August, 2003.[1]

Benefits for Communities

Some 22 states now have commercial-scale wind farms feeding electricity into the grid. Although there occasionally is a NIMBY ["not in my backyard"] problem, the PIIMBY response ("put it in my backyard") is much more pervasive. This is not surprising, since a single turbine easily can produce $100,000 worth of electricity in a year.

The competition among farmers in Iowa or ranchers in Colorado for wind farms is intense. Farmers, with no investment on their part, typically receive $3,000 a year in royalties from the local utility for siting a single wind turbine, which occupies a quarter-acre of land. This quarter-acre in corn country would produce 40 bushels worth $120; in ranch country, perhaps $10 worth of beef.

Communities in rural America desperately want the additional revenue from wind farms and the jobs they bring. Moreover, money spent on electricity generated from wind farms stays in the community, creating a ripple effect throughout the local economy. Within a matter of years, thousands of ranchers could be earning far more from electricity sales than from cattle.

Moving to the highly efficient gas-electric hybrids with a plug-in capability, combined with the construction of thousands of wind farms across the country feeding electricity into a national grid, will provide the energy security that has eluded us for three decades. It also will rejuvenate farm and ranch communities and shrink the U.S. balance-of-trade deficit. Even more important, it dramatically will cut carbon emissions, making the U.S. a model that other countries can emulate.

1. This blackout—the largest in American history affected—millions of people in both Canada and the United States. Many people charge that it was the result of an aging and overloaded electricity system.

> "The 21st-century science of nanotechnology has possibilities only limited by one's imagination."

Nanotechnology Will Benefit Americans in the Twenty-First Century

Morgan O'Rourke

In the following viewpoint Morgan O'Rourke maintains that nanotechnology, the manipulation of materials at the atomic and molecular level, could help improve life for Americans in the twenty-first century. While more research needs to be conducted to assess the risks associated with this technology, says O'Rourke, it holds unlimited potential for new product development and will also lead to advances in medicine and conservation. O'Rourke is the managing editor of *Risk Management*, a monthly magazine that offers analysis on the risks of existing and emerging technology.

As you read, consider the following questions:

1. As explained by O'Rourke, how can nanotechnology help prevent pollution?
2. According to the author, how much of President Bush's 2005 federal budget was allocated to nanotechnology science?
3. How did Michael Crichton's novel contribute to fear of nanotechnology, as explained by O'Rourke?

Morgan O'Rourke, "Smaller and Smaller and Smaller: Examining the Possibilities of Nanotechnology," *Risk Management*, vol. 51, August 2004, pp. 38–42. Copyright © 2004 by Risk Management Society Publishing, Inc. Reproduced by permission.

"**I**magine a medical device that travels through the human body to seek out and destroy small clusters of cancerous cells before they can spread. Or a box no larger than a sugar cube that contains the entire contents of the Library of Congress. Or materials much lighter than steel that possess 10 times as much strength."

An Infinitesimally Small Scale

As the above quote from the National Science Foundation suggests, the 21st-century science of nanotechnology has possibilities only limited by one's imagination. Nanotechnology, which refers to the manipulation of materials at the atomic and molecular level, could allow scientists to create almost anything from sunscreens to the smallest, most powerful computers using the most basic of nature's building blocks. The potential is so vast that the National Science Foundation estimates that worldwide revenues from nanotechnology-based products and innovations in areas such as materials, electronics, pharmaceuticals, chemicals, aerospace, tools, healthcare and sustainability will exceed $1 trillion by 2015. . . .

The term "nanotechnology" is derived from the Greek root "nanos," meaning dwarf. While an appropriate starting point, this does not begin to adequately describe the scale that researchers in this field are dealing with. Consider that a human hair has a width of about 90,000 nanometers while the head of a pin has a width of more than one million nanometers. Nanotechnology, by contrast, is concerned with materials that are anywhere from one to 100 nanometers wide.

Thus researchers are working on an infinitesimally small level that has only recently been made possible with the advent of sophisticated tools, such as the scanning tunneling microscope and the atomic force microscope. These devices not only allow scientists to examine samples at the molecular and atomic level but also allow them to manipulate microscopic particles on a surface and take computer images of the results for further study.

Unlimited Potential

Currently, nanotechnology research has advanced to the point where scientists can study the effects of molecular manipulation but, for the most part, are unable to create new and sophisticated commercial products. However, even the ability to move and position atomic particles is a breakthrough because these materials are the basic building blocks of all matter. Many researchers believe that mastering particle manipulation on this level will allow them to create almost anything. It will simply be a matter of putting the right materials in the correct place to achieve the desired result. For instance, Eric Drexler, one of the founders of the Foresight Institute, a Palo Alto, California–based nonprofit nanotechnology education organization, has theorized that with the correct positioning of particles, nanotechnology could create a steak from grass, water and foodstuffs without ever involving a cow at all. Or it could create smaller, more efficient machines by densely packing the required materials in smaller and smaller surface areas, rendering Moore's Law of computer power advancement (which states that available processing power doubles every 18 months) virtually obsolete.

Christine Peterson, president of the Foresight Institute, sees potential in the development of nanomachines that can lead to advances in medicine and environmental cleanup. "In medicine, [nanotechnology] combines the benefits of surgery and drugs in the same unit," she says. "You get the chemical reaction of drugs with the three-dimensional control of surgery all the way down at the nanoscale. If you have this, you could go in and fix any problem that you have in terms of physical medicine."

By controlling processes at a molecular level, products that do not contribute to pollution are also possible, says Peterson. "You can manufacture things with no chemical pollution because you have total control of the atoms in the process." This means that waste can be controlled or even eliminated altogether. Nanomachines can also be created to break down existing pollutants, making remediation efforts easier.

"This kind of nanotechnology is biotech without the bio," says Peterson. "It is that scale and that power without the limitations of the biological system. The principle is total control at the molecular level, building whatever is physically possible to exist and that we can understand and design within software limitations."

These major innovations are years away, however. Today, nanotechnology appears in computer hard drives, which contain giant magnetoresistance heads that allow for increased storage capacity through nano-thin layers of magnetic materials. Self-cleaning windows utilize coatings of microscopic hydrophobic particles that repel water and dirt from the surface of the glass. And in the department store, nanotechnology comes into play in wrinkle- and stain-resistant clothing, which is created from fabrics coated with microscopic materials that create a thin cushion of air above the cotton fabric that smooths out the wrinkles and allows liquids to bead up and roll off the surface of a new pair of khakis, for instance. Other applications already seeing commercial development include automotive sensors, landmine detectors, burn and wound dressings, water filtration, dental-bonding agents, car bumpers, sunscreens and cosmetics, and light-weight tennis racquets and durable tennis balls. Although these products might seem relatively commonplace, they would have been considered space-age only a few years ago.

Revolutionizing Manufacturing

Nano-manufacturing will be available from common elements already in your own backyard, at little or no cost. Nano-assemblers will move atoms and nanorobots at the atomic level and allow for the creation of any commodity you can possibly dream about. . . . Food could be replicated. Starvation and hunger could be eliminated from the globe. Homelessness can disappear: program the nano-assemblers and watch them construct a mansion before your very eyes, using atoms like those found in wood linking them in the correct atomic sequences. Manufacturing comprised from simple soil in one's own backyard, would yield almost any commodity. This means raw material extraction, currently necessary and contracted globally, would not be required. Most needed atoms and raw material can be extracted with a wheel barrow and a shovel at home in your backyard. This could potentially change the shape of all global manufacturing and trade.

Robert W.S. Dunkley, *Futures*, December 2004.

The U.S. government also understands the potential of nanotechnology and has made significant investments in it. In the 2005 federal budget, President [George W.] Bush requested nearly $1 billion to be allocated for nanoscale science, engineering and technology. According to the National Nanotechnology Initiative, this funding will be used primarily for a variety of initiatives including:

- research to uncover new phenomena and properties of materials at the nanoscale
- research to enable the nanoscale as the most efficient manufacturing domain
- developing more sensitive and sophisticated techniques for detecting and protecting against chemical, biological, radiological and nuclear weaponry
- nano-biosystems and medicine . . .
- development of instrumentation and standards
- environmental and health issues
- education and training for the new generation of workers
- partnerships to enhance industrial participation in the nanotechnological revolution

Exploring the Risks

As the use of nanotechnology increases, it will be increasingly important to assess the risks involved. But since the science is ever-changing, many of these questions have yet to be answered. "The mere presence of nanoparticles does not pose a threat to people or the environment," says Annabelle Hett of Swiss Re's Risk Engineering Services division. "A risk can only arise if some of the particles' properties turn out to be harmful. However, insufficient research has been done to say with any certainty whether, and if so to what extent, nanoparticles or products containing nanoparticles actually pose a threat.". . .

Quite possibly one of biggest hurdles for the field of nanotechnology and, in turn, for insurers and risk managers looking to accurately assess risk and potential liability, is one of image and reputation.

Science fiction has had its way with nanotechnology and, in some cases, has created an unnecessary and unwarranted cloud of panic around the subject.

In Michael Crichton's 2002 novel *Prey* nanotechnology is responsible for microscopic self-replicating robots that turn on their creators in a murderous rampage. Although a work of fiction, the book introduced many people to a worst-case scenario that has actually gained a foothold in the public nanotech debate. The fear of a takeover by hostile, self-replicating nanomachines—termed "grey goo"—has been dismissed by many serious researchers, however. . . .

The challenge for the manufacturers and consumers of nanotechnology-based products will be to not only overcome the unfounded Hollywood-style fears and assumptions that some people may have already formulated, but to deal with the serious issues of nanotechnology and its application. This is a task that will require a proactive approach from the industry with clear and timely communication from all involved parties in order to correctly inform the public to the true measure of the risk associated with these products. And should certain products prove faulty—as new technology often does—speedy and efficient product recall strategies and public information campaigns will be even more important to prevent reputational damage.

With the potential for countless product liability situations, nanotech products, like any new product, must undergo extensive testing before they can enter the commercial market. "The way that people should think about this is the way they do with any chemicals," says Peterson. "We should treat them the way we do any new chemical, especially anything that you put on the body that could be absorbed." Peterson points out that testing efforts have lagged behind because many of the materials that nanotechnology researchers work with are known quantities already proven safe. But when these materials are reduced to a nanoscale they can behave much differently than they did before. Colors and properties change. Insulating materials become conductive. And possibly, harmless substances could become toxic. "So we have to think of them as a new chemical," says Peterson. "We will have to start over with the standard procedures."

A Significant Role in the Future

While the study of nanotechnology raises many-challenging questions, its potential means that the science will continue to move forward. "Nanotechnology makes possible a large number of innovative products that are attractive to consumers and beneficial to the environment," says Bruno Porro, chief risk officer of Swiss Re. "The trend towards miniaturization also carries within it a potential for growth, which analysts say will be of major economic significance in the next few years."

"Exploration and discovery are key agents of growth in society—technologically, economically, socially, internationally, and intellectually."

Space Exploration Will Play an Important Role in America's Future

National Aeronautics and Space Administration

The following viewpoint is excerpted from a 2004 publication by the National Aeronautics and Space Administration (NASA). The agency argues that space exploration will play an important role in America's future. According to NASA, this exploration will stimulate the development of critical technologies and encourage young Americans to pursue careers in science and engineering, careers that are critical to America's future financial competitiveness. NASA believes that space exploration will also inspire both Americans and others around the world and will answer important questions about the human experience. NASA, established in 1958, is the government agency responsible for America's space program and long-term aerospace research.

As you read, consider the following questions:

1. What recent new discoveries have revolutionized science's understanding of the universe, according to NASA?
2. According to the author, how does research for space exploration impact the economy and national security?
3. How can space exploration inspire children, in the opinion of NASA?

National Aeronautics and Space Administration, "The Vision for Space Exploration," www.nasa.gov, February 2004.

Understanding from the unknown. Comprehension from the cosmos. Insight from the infinite. The relationship between discovery and exploration has driven human curiosity for all of recorded history. Since the time of the ancient philosophers, we have striven to comprehend our place in the universe and have looked to the heavens for answers to the questions: Where do we come from? Are we alone? Where are we going?

Exploration and discovery have been especially important to the American experience. New World pioneers and American frontiersmen showed our Nation the importance of the knowledge, technology, resources, and inspiration that flow from exploration. Like the ancients, America has also explored the heavens, and in the latter half of the 20th century, the Apollo Moon landings became the most distant milestone in the continuing American exploratory tradition.

A Pivotal Time in History

At the beginning of the 21st century, we stand at a unique time in our exploration of the heavens. The exploratory voyages of the next few decades have the potential—within our lifetimes—to answer age-old questions about how life begins, whether life exists elsewhere, and how we could live out there.

Our understanding of the universe and its habitability is being revolutionized by new discoveries. Scientists have found new forms of life in environments once thought inhospitable. Spacecraft have identified potential new resources on the Moon. Robotic probes have found evidence of water, a key ingredient of life, on the planet Mars. A mission to Jupiter has revealed that oceans likely underlay the icy surfaces of that planet's moons. Astronomers have discovered over 100 planets, and counting, circling other stars. Together, these findings indicate that our universe may be more habitable than previously known. Instead of a dry, lifeless universe, there may be many worlds that harbored life in the past and can support life today.

We also stand at a pivotal time in the history of human space flight, when important choices about investments in the Space Shuttle, the International Space Station, and follow-on programs are being made in the wake of the Space

Shuttle *Columbia* tragedy.[1] Just as decisions to begin the Space Station and Space Shuttle programs were made 20 and 30 years ago, the direction we set for our human space flight programs today will define space exploration for decades to come.

The President's Vision for space exploration is bold and forward-thinking. It expands scientific discovery and the search for habitable environments and life by advancing human and robotic capabilities across multiple worlds. . . . It seeks to establish a sustainable and flexible approach to exploration by pursuing compelling questions, developing breakthrough technologies, leveraging space resources, and making smart decisions about ongoing programs. It will help drive critical national technologies in power, computing, nanotechnology, biotechnology, communications, networking, robotics, and materials. It will start exciting new programs now to inspire the next generation of explorers. . . .

NASA Guiding Principles for Exploration

Pursue Compelling Questions

Exploration of the solar system and beyond will be guided by compelling questions of scientific and societal importance. NASA exploration programs will seek profound answers to questions about the origins of our solar system, whether life exists beyond Earth, and how we could live on other worlds.

Across Multiple Worlds

NASA will make progress across a broad front of destinations, starting with a return to the Moon to enable future human exploration of Mars and other worlds. Consistent with recent discoveries, NASA will focus on possible habitable environments on Mars, the moons of Jupiter, and in other solar systems. Where advantageous, NASA will also make use of destinations like the Moon and near-Earth asteroids to test and demonstrate new exploration capabilities.

Employ Human and Robotic Capabilities

NASA will send human and robotic explorers as partners, leveraging the capabilities of each where most useful. Robotic

---

1. On February 1, 2003, *Columbia* disintegrated during re-entry on its twenty-eighth mission, killing all seven crew members aboard.

explorers will visit new worlds first, to obtain scientific data, assess risks to our astronauts, demonstrate breakthrough technologies, identify space resources, and send tantalizing imagery back to Earth. Human explorers will follow to conduct in-depth research, direct and upgrade advanced robotic explorers, prepare space resources, and demonstrate new exploration capabilities.

For Sustainable Exploration

NASA will pursue breakthrough technologies, investigate lunar and other space resources, and align ongoing programs to develop sustainable, affordable, and flexible solar system exploration strategies.

Use the Moon as a Testing Ground for Mars and Beyond

Under this new Vision, the first robotic missions will be sent to the Moon as early as 2008 and the first human missions as early as 2015 to test new approaches, systems and operations for sustainable human and robotic missions to Mars and beyond.

Starting Now

NASA will pursue this Vision as our highest priority. Consistent with the FY [fiscal year] 2005 Budget, NASA will immediately begin to realign programs and organization, demonstrate new technical capabilities, and undertake new robotic precursor missions to the Moon and Mars before the end of the decade.

Exploration Roadmap

Over the next three decades, NASA will send robotic probes to explore our solar system, including our Earth's Moon, the planet Mars, the moons of Jupiter and other outer planets, and will launch new space telescopes to search for planets beyond our solar system. These robotic explorers will pursue compelling scientific questions, demonstrate breakthrough technologies, identify space resources, and extend an advanced telepresence that will send stunning imagery back to Earth.

Starting at the Moon in 2008 and at Mars in 2011, NASA will launch dedicated robotic missions that will demonstrate new technologies and enhance our scientific knowledge of these destinations. These new technologies and discoveries will pave the way for more capable robotic missions and eventually human missions. The first human explorers will be sent to the Moon as early as 2015, as a stepping stone to demonstrate sustainable approaches to exploring Mars and other worlds.

A Human Imperative

For what, today, do we recall renaissance Spain, King Ferdinand, and Queen Isabella? Unless one is a professional historian, the memory which is evoked is their sponsorship of [explorer Christopher] Columbus in his voyages of discovery. For what, in five hundred years, will our era be recalled? We will never know, but I believe it will be for the Apollo lunar landings if for anything at all. And this is entirely appropriate. Human expansion into space is a continuation of the ancient human imperative to explore, to exploit, to settle new territory when and as it becomes possible to do so. This imperative will surely be satisfied, by others if not by us.

We know this, if not with our logic then with our intuition. We are all the descendants of people who left known and familiar places to strike out for the risky promise of better places, in an unbroken chain going back to a small corner of east Africa. Concerning the settlement of the American West, it has been said that "the cowards never started, and the weaklings died on the way." But this has been true of every human migration; we are all the descendants of those who chose to explore and to settle new lands, and who survived the experience.

Michael D. Griffin, congressional testimony, October 16, 2003.

To support these missions, a number of key building blocks are necessary. These include new capabilities in propulsion, power, communications, crew transport, and launch, as well as the refocusing of ongoing programs like Space Station research. Major achievements, including the completion of Space Station assembly, test flights of new crew transport capabilities, and space technology demonstrations, are expected before the end of this decade. . . .

National Benefits

Just as [explorers] Meriwether Lewis and William Clark could not have predicted the settlement of the American

West within a hundred years of the start of their famous 19th century expedition, the total benefits of a single exploratory undertaking or discovery cannot be predicted in advance. Because the very purpose of exploratory voyages and research is to understand the unknown, exact benefits defy calculation. Nonetheless, we can define important categories of benefits to the Nation and society.

Preparing for exploration and research accelerates the development of technologies that are important to the economy and national security. The space missions in this plan require advanced systems and capabilities that will accelerate the development of many critical technologies, including power, computing, nanotechnology, biotechnology, communications, networking, robotics, and materials. These technologies underpin and advance the U.S. economy and help ensure national security. NASA plans to work with other government agencies and the private sector to develop space systems that can address national and commercial needs.

Space exploration holds a special place in the human imagination. Youth are especially drawn to Mars rovers, astronauts, and telescopes. If engaged effectively and creatively, space inspires children to seek careers in math, science, and engineering, careers that are critical to our future national economic competitiveness.

The accomplishments of U.S. space explorers are also a particularly potent symbol of American democracy, a reminder of what the human spirit can achieve in a free society. However, space exploration also encourages international cooperation, where spacecraft and explorers come to represent our world as well as our Nation.

When the unknown becomes known, it catalyzes change, stimulating human thought, creativity and imagination. The scientific questions that this plan pursues have the potential to revolutionize whole fields of research. For example, scientists are still working to understand how similarly sized planets, such as Mars and Earth, could have developed so differently and what that could mean for our planet. If life is found beyond Earth, biological processes on other worlds may be very different from those evolved on our world. Outside the sciences, the very knowledge that life exists elsewhere in the universe may hold revelations for fields in the humanities.

Exploration and discovery are key agents of growth in society—technologically, economically, socially, internationally, and intellectually. This plan sets in motion activities that will contribute to change and growth in the U.S. and the world over the next century.

Periodical Bibliography

The following articles have been selected to supplement the diverse views presented in this chapter.

Harold W. Baillie	"Genetic Engineering and Our Human Nature," *Philosophy & Public Policy Quarterly*, Winter/Spring 2003.
Stephen Baker and Adam Aston	"Why the Old Rules Don't Apply: At This Size, Familiar Materials Can Do Things They Couldn't Do Before," *Business Week*, February 14, 2005.
Mathew Cabot	"Tomorrow's Treatments," *Natural Science*, March 2001.
Jonathan Coleman	"Is Technology Making Us Intimate Strangers?" *Newsweek*, March 27, 2000.
Economist	"Frankenfood Approved: GM Farming," March 13, 2004.
Economist	"The Men in White Coats Are Winning, Slowly—Non-food GM," October 2, 2004.
Jonathan Fahey	"Hydrogen Gas," *Forbes*, April 25, 2005.
Peter Hoffmann	"The Hydrogen Power Rush," *World & I*, October 2002.
M. Therese Lysaught	"Let's Make the World a No-Clone Zone," *U.S. Catholic*, April 2003.
Michael Marriot	"Toys Today, Servants Tomorrow," *New York Times*, March 22, 2001.
New Scientist	"From Atoms to Engines: The History of Nanotechnology," March 5, 2005.
Nancy Scheper-Hughes	"Postmodern Cannibalism," *Whole Earth*, Summer 2000.
Luba Vangelova	"True or False? Extinction Is Forever," *Smithsonian*, June 2003.
Todd Woody	"Should We Clone Fading Species?" *Popular Science*, July 2003.
Jack Yamaduchi	"Hydrogen Power for the Masses," *Automotive Engineering International*, January 2005.

CHAPTER 3

How Can Life for Americans Be Improved?

Chapter Preface

The year 2004 marked the fortieth anniversary of the Civil Rights Act of 1964, a landmark piece of legislation that outlawed many forms of discrimination and segregation based on race. This law marked a fundamental shift toward racial equality for African Americans in the United States. However, while it resulted in many positive changes, many analysts contend that for a large proportion of African Americans, racial inequality persists. Many people maintain that this inequality is a serious problem in American society and believe it is one of many problems that need to be addressed to improve life in the United States.

Numerous national statistics show that great disparities exist between whites and African Americans in economics, housing, education, social justices, and civic engagement. For example, according to a 2004 report by the National Urban League, less than 50 percent of African American families own their own homes, versus 70 percent for whites. The league also found that African Americans are denied mortgages and home improvement loans at twice the rate of whites. Figures published by the Bureau of Labor Statistics show similar discrepancies in employment. In 2003 the average unemployment rate for white workers was 4.9 percent, but for African Americans it was between 9.8 and 11 percent.

There is widespread disagreement on how such disparities can be reduced. Some people believe that racial segregation results in prejudice and unequal treatment of African Americans and that efforts to reduce inequality must thus focus on desegregation of communities and schools. Researcher Marc Seitles explains: "When a community is racially diverse, the people who live there have an opportunity to learn tolerance, which in turn may lessen the extent to which minorities are subject to all forms of prejudice." According to Seitles, "Segregation . . . fosters racial stereotypes and myths that minorities are less intelligent, lazy, and inferior. . . . The only way to combat these misconceptions, fears, and stereotypes is through increased association between blacks, whites, and other minorities, leading to a better understanding between racial groups and greater racial equality."

Other commentators argue that inequality has been caused by a history of public assistance to whites but not to African Americans. Betsey Leondar-Wright, a communications director at the United for a Fair Economy organization, likens the path to prosperity in America to a staircase. "For most white men, the staircase has been an escalator powered by public assistance," she says. In contrast, "For people of color, the escalator has been broken." She adds, "Sometimes they have had to hike up a down escalator." In her opinion, blacks "rarely got the same rewards as white people. Their wages were lower, and many neighborhoods and schools were closed to them. In some eras and places, laws and violence kept them off the staircase to prosperity entirely." Leondar-Wright and others argue that in order to achieve equality, this trend of unequal assistance must be halted.

Racial inequality is not the only problem plaguing American society in the twenty-first century, of course. The following chapter explores diverse opinions on how life for Americans can be improved by making changes to health care, immigration policies, education, and social security.

"Insurance premiums are exploding, and the system of employment-linked insurance is falling apart."

America Should Move Toward a Socialized Health Care System

Paul Krugman

America's employment-based system of health insurance is expensive and ineffective, maintains Paul Krugman in the following viewpoint. In Krugman's opinion, the current system fails because private companies raise costs to compensate for high-risk patients. He believes a socialized health care system—where the government assumes more risks—would be far more effective, and he argues that the United States should take steps toward developing such a system. Krugman is a columnist for the *New York Times* and professor of economics and international affairs at Princeton University. He is the author or editor of twenty books and more than two hundred papers in professional journals and edited volumes.

As you read, consider the following questions:

1. According to the author, how have rising health care costs affected the number of uninsured in the United States?
2. As cited by Krugman, how much does the United States spend on health care per capita compared with Canada?
3. How does the United States compare with other countries when health care success is measured, according to the author?

Working Americans have two great concerns: the growing difficulty of getting health insurance, and the continuing difficulty they have in finding jobs. These concerns may have a common cause: soaring insurance premiums.

An Employment-Based System

In most advanced countries, the government provides everyone with health insurance. In America, however, the government offers insurance only if you're elderly (Medicare) or poor (Medicaid). Otherwise, you're expected to get private health insurance, usually through your job. But insurance premiums are exploding, and the system of employment-linked insurance is falling apart.

Some employers have dropped their health plans. Others have maintained benefits for current workers, but are finding ways to avoid paying benefits to new hires—for example, by using temporary workers. And some businesses, while continuing to provide health benefits, are refusing to hire more workers.

In other words, rising health care costs aren't just causing a rapid rise in the ranks of the uninsured (confirmed by yesterday's [August 26, 2004] Census Bureau report); they're also, because of their link to employment, a major reason why this economic recovery has generated fewer jobs than any previous economic expansion.

Clearly, health care reform is an urgent social and economic issue. But who has the right answer?

The 2004 Economic Report of the President told us what George [W.] Bush's economists think, though we're unlikely to hear anything as blunt at next week's convention. According to the report, health costs are too high because people have too much insurance and purchase too much medical care. What we need, then, are policies, like tax-advantaged health savings accounts tied to plans with high deductibles, that induce people to pay more of their medical expenses out of pocket. (Cynics would say that this is just a rationale for yet another tax shelter for the wealthy, but the economists who wrote the report are probably sincere.)

[Democratic 2004 presidential nominee] John Kerry's economic advisers have a very different analysis: they believe that health costs are too high because private insurance companies have excessive overhead, mainly because they are trying to avoid covering high-risk patients. What we need, according to this view, is for the government to assume more of the risk, for example by picking up catastrophic health costs, thereby reducing the incentive for socially wasteful spending, and making employment-based insurance easier to get.

Reasons Why Uninsured Workers Lack Employer-Sponsored Insurance, 2001

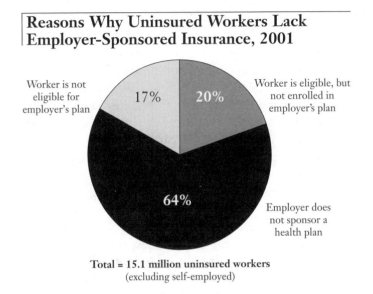

Worker is not eligible for employer's plan — 17%

Worker is eligible, but not enrolled in employer's plan — 20%

Employer does not sponsor a health plan — 64%

Total = 15.1 million uninsured workers
(excluding self-employed)

Note: Percentages do not total 100% due to rounding.

Kaiser Commission on Medicaid and the Uninsured, 2004. www.kff.org.

A smart economist can come up with theoretical justifications for either argument. The evidence suggests, however, that the Kerry position is much closer to the truth.

The fact is that the mainly private U.S. health care system spends far more than the mainly public health care systems of other advanced countries, but gets worse results. In 2001, we spent $4,887 on health care per capita, compared with $2,792 in Canada and $2,561 in France. Yet the U.S. does worse than either country by any measure of health care success you care to name—life expectancy, infant mortality, whatever. (At its best, U.S. health care is the best in the world. But the ranks of Americans who can't afford the best, and may have no insurance at all, are large and growing.)

And the U.S. system does have very high overhead: private insurers and H.M.O's [health maintenance organizations] spend much more on administrative expenses, as opposed to actual medical treatment, than public agencies at home or abroad.

Socialized Health Care

Does this mean that the American way is wrong, and that we should switch to a Canadian-style single-payer system? Well, yes. Put it this way: in Canada, respectable business executives are ardent defenders of "socialized medicine." Two years ago [in 2002] the Conference Board of Canada—a who's who of the nation's corporate elite—issued a report urging fellow Canadians to bear in mind not just the "symbolic value" of universal health care, but its "economic contribution to the competitiveness of Canadian businesses."

My health-economist friends say that it's unrealistic to call for a single-payer system here: the interest groups are too powerful, and the antigovernment propaganda of the right has become too well established in public opinion. All that we can hope for right now is a modest step in the right direction. . . . I bow to their political wisdom. But let's not ignore the growing evidence that our dysfunctional medical system is bad not just for our health, but for our economy.

"When the effects of socialized medical programs are measured . . . it is hard to show any effect on any health outcome."

America's Health Care System Should Not Be Socialized

Jane Orient

In the following viewpoint physician Jane Orient argues that while America's health care system does need to be fixed, a socialized system is not the answer. There is no evidence that socialized medicine results in better health care, maintains Orient, and there is no proof that it would be beneficial for the government to assume the risk for catastrophic health care costs. Instead, she says, a socialized system would impose unfair government controls on both individuals and the health care system. Orient is executive director of the Association of American Physicians and Surgeons.

As you read, consider the following questions:

1. Why are infant mortality statistics between countries not comparable, according to Orient?
2. How would a socialized system impact doctors' earnings, in the author's view?
3. What does Orient imply about government spending on administrative costs?

Jane Orient, "America Needs Socialized Medicine? It Just Ain't So!" *The Freeman: Ideas on Liberty*, January/February 2005, pp. 6–7. Copyright © 2005 by Foundation for Economic Education, Inc., www.fee.org. All rights reserved. Reproduced by permission.

[Journalist] Paul Krugman attributes "America's Failing Health" to the lack of Canadian-style socialized medicine and thus to the persistence of a free-enterprise sector in American medicine.

Because "interest groups are too powerful, and the antigovernment propaganda of the right has become too well established," his prescription is a "modest step in the right direction," rather than a one-step enactment of a Canadian system.

A Socialized System Will Not Work

Let's see now: the United States has been taking such "modest steps" toward socialized medicine since the 1940s. There was Hill-Burton, or federal aid to build hospitals, in 1946; Kerr-Mills, to provide federal aid to elderly who couldn't afford needed medical care, in 1960; then Medicare in 1965, and Medicaid.

In the [Bill] Clinton years, there were additional modest steps, notably the State Children's Health Insurance Program (SCHIP). And George W. Bush brought us another try at a Medicare prescription-drug benefit, which is to be implemented in 2006—unless there's a replay of seniors' reactions to the last attempt to introduce a prescription-drug benefit in 1989, when the seniors assaulted Rep. Dan Rostenkowski's car.

What has been the result of these incremental intrusions into American medicine? An ever-increasing number of uninsured? A noncompetitive automobile industry? An overall drag on the economy?

Why, no. Those are mere temporal associations. Correlation doesn't prove causation. The real explanation is that there hasn't been *enough* federal intervention, in Krugman's view. The remnant of a private sector competing with the government for those scarce resources is, paradoxically, the cause of the problems.

Scarce resources? Not exactly. In the United States it is said we spend *too much* on medical care, but there is a misallocation of the resources. That's because selfish people want too much medical care for themselves and their families, and greedy doctors and hospitals want to provide too much treatment to those who can pay for it.

What we need, Krugman apparently supposes, is an infallible government planning mechanism to divide up the resources and to put a rigid ceiling on spending, and nongreedy doctors and hospitals to allocate the available care in the fairest possible way. Public-spirited doctors and hospitals will replace the ones we have now as soon as all their checks start coming from the government.

And of course the government will allocate a lot of resources to providing health care to healthy people, whether they want it or not (especially mental-health care), to keep them healthy. If some people get sick before all ill-health is prevented and end up circling emergency rooms in an ambulance or parked in a corridor, that will keep the pressure on for more spending.

When the effects of socialized medical programs are measured in a way that controls for confounding variables (like educational level and drug abuse), it is hard to show any effect on any health outcome, such as low birth weight. If one compares infant mortality in Canadian and American Indians of the same genetic stock, however, the Americans do better.

But the big picture, Krugman claims, is lower infant mortality and longer life expectancy in a number of countries that have socialized medicine. In this case, correlation *does* prove causation, Krugman implies—even if the statistics aren't comparable. (Since very low-birth-weight babies are considered stillbirths in some socialized countries, whereas they are counted as live births here, the United States looks worse—even though many more tiny preemies survive here.)

Krugman may call his proposal a "modest step." But the incremental march toward socialism is the way to bring about revolutionary changes. It is hardly less modest than [author] Jonathan Swift's [satirical] proposal to solve the Irish famine problem by eating babies. And if the Krugman Plan were presented honestly, it might provoke a similar reaction.

What to Look Forward To

This is what "single payer" Canadian-style socialism would mean:

- Everyone is forced to pay, through taxes, for other people's "health care," especially for their well-baby vis-

its, mental-health screening, contraceptives, steriliza-
tions, or other politically favored services.

- No one is permitted to pay for "covered" medical care for himself or a family member, unless the family member is a dog or a cat.
- No medical practitioner or facility is permitted to earn a profit by providing more sophisticated, more convenient, or more effective care.
- Doctors' total earnings are capped, so that if they do more than the maximum permitted amount of work, it will be at their own expense.
- The availability of care is totally controlled by a political process.
- Employers and employees get to unload the entire burden of medical insurance onto taxpayers, dragging down the entire economy instead of individual industries that have succumbed to Big-Labor demands for unaffordable benefits.
- The Medicare Pac-Man will devour the entire federal treasury even sooner, unless there are massive cuts in promised benefits.
- The sick must compete with the healthy and the well-connected for a share of politically rational resources.

A Free Market System

America's health care policy stands at the crossroads. Either we are going to continue the slow march toward a government-driven system, or we are going to choose a free market solution that puts consumers in charge. The governmental system ultimately will lead to less choice and a stifling of innovation. The free market solution will enable America to solve its health care cost problem and capture the promise of twenty-first-century medicine: a promise of new cures for diseases, longer lives made possible by the mapping of the human genome, and nanotechnology.

John F. Cogan, R. Glenn Hubbard, and Daniel P. Kessler, *Wall Street Journal*, May 4, 2004.

Honest description, however, is not to be expected of socialists. Krugman, for example, says that the government "offers" insurance to the elderly. The fact is that the day

Medicare took effect, [then–U.S. president] Lyndon Johnson got all insurers to cancel existing health benefits for the elderly. One can decline to accept Medicare Part B (physician coverage), for which there is no private substitute, but the only way to avoid Medicare Part A (hospital coverage) is to give up all Social Security benefits. Thus a correct description would be: "The U.S. forces the elderly to depend on the federal government for health insurance."

Government Control Is Not the Answer

Krugman likes the idea of having the government "assume the risk" for catastrophic health costs, "thereby reducing the incentive for socially wasteful spending." Translated, this means having the government take over all true medical insurance (which is meant to cover catastrophes, not routine expenses) and enabling the government to ration expensive care to the sick.

Krugman repeats the assertions that government health insurance—unlike the Post Office and the Pentagon—has less overhead than private enterprise. It is remotely possible that Medicare spends less on administration than some private insurers, although a 1994 study by the Council for Affordable Health Insurance showed that private insurers spend less. Nobody really knows because government accounting makes Enron's look like a model of simplicity and honesty.[1]

Moreover, Medicare imposes tremendously costly burdens on "providers."

Krugman is right in his assessment that there is much wrong with the status quo. The system of third-party payment is upside down and backwards. But instead of rebuilding the foundation, the Krugman solution would kick out the props, hastening the collapse of an unwieldy monster and crushing the best of medical care in the process.

---

1. In 2001 Enron filed for bankruptcy after high-level corruption, accounting errors, and insider trading were revealed to be taking place.

"What we should do is call a halt to the current heedless increase in annual immigration."

Strict Limits Should Be Imposed on Immigration

Steven A. Camarota

Current levels of immigration to the United States have reached an all-time high, argues Steven A. Camarota in the following viewpoint. He asserts that increased immigration is harming American society. Immigrants increase poverty rates, raise health insurance costs, and strain educational resources, he maintains. In addition, says Camarota, a steady influx of immigrants means that the majority of them are failing to assimilate into American society. He advocates a drastic decrease in U.S. immigration quotas so that there is time to assimilate those people already living in the country. Camarota is director of research for the Center for Immigration Studies, a think tank devoted to research and analysis of the impact of immigration on the United States.

As you read, consider the following questions:
1. How does immigration drive up the cost of health insurance, as argued by Camarota?
2. According to the author, why are schools failing to help immigrant children assimilate?
3. In Camarota's opinion, to what annual rate should the United States reduce immigration?

When the history of the 1990s is written, the most important story may not be the GOP [Republican Party] takeover of Congress, the boom economy, or the [Bill] Clinton impeachment. The big story may be the decade's unprecedented level of immigration: a social phenomenon of enormous significance, affecting everything from the nation's schools to the political balance between the two parties.

Newly released census figures show that the foreign-born population reached 31.1 million in 2000 (including some 7 to 8 million here illegally). This is by far the largest immigrant population in U.S. history, and represents a 57 percent increase from 1990. The rate of increase is itself unprecedented: Even during the great wave of immigration from 1900 to 1910, the foreign-born population grew by only about 31 percent (from roughly 10 million to 13.5 million). Over the past 30 years, the number of immigrants in the U.S. has tripled. If current trends are allowed to continue, the foreign-born share of the population will in fact pass the all-time high by the end of this decade. Many defenders of high immigration argue that the current immigration is not really unusual, because although the numbers and growth are without precedent, the total U.S. population was smaller 100 years ago and immigrants constituted a larger share of the total. It is true that the 11.1 percent of the nation's population that is foreign-born today is lower than the all-time high of nearly 15 percent reached in 1910. But one may ask why 1910 should be the benchmark by which to judge today's immigration. In evaluating its effect on modern society, it seems more reasonable to compare today's immigration with that of the more recent past. And in that context, today's figures represent a fundamental break with prior decades: From 1940 to 1990, the foreign-born population averaged less than 7 percent, and as recently as 1970 it was less than 5 percent.

Serious Implications

The implications for American society are enormous. For example, a good deal of attention has been given to the fact that the number of people who live in poverty did not decline in the 1990s, despite a strong economy. What has generally not been reported is that new immigrants and their U.S.-born children accounted for the nation's stubborn poverty rate. The primary reason so many immigrant families live in poverty is that a large percentage have very little education. Newly arrived adult immigrants, for example, are more than three times as likely as natives to lack a high-school education.

Immigrants and their children also account for nearly two-thirds of the increase in the population lacking health insurance over the last decade. By dramatically increasing the uninsured population, immigration creates significant costs for taxpayers, and it drives up costs for insured Americans as providers pass along the costs of treating the uninsured to paying customers. The central role immigration has played in creating the nation's health-insurance quandary has largely gone unreported.

Ignoring Public Opinion

Immigration has a profound impact on the issues that Americans say matter most to them. Concerns about national security, the quality of education, high tax burdens, urban sprawl, and many other "front burner" issues are directly affected by an influx of more than one million immigrants annually. The U.S. Census Bureau projects that, left unchecked, immigration will be the principal cause of a 50 percent increase in our population during the first half of the 21st century. A factor that important to our national future deserves comprehensive and thoughtful consideration by the people's elected representatives. Yet while poll after poll shows that the public is anxious to consider a wide array of immigration reforms, legal and illegal immigration continue to careen out of control.

Federation for American Immigration Reform, September 2003.
www.fairus.org.

The impact on public schools is even more significant. In the last 20 years the school-age population has grown by roughly 8 million. Most observers agree that this increase has strained resources in districts across the country. What most media accounts of this growth leave out is that census data indicate that there are about 8 million school-age children from immigrant families—and, because they are much poorer on average than natives, this increase in enrollment has not been accompanied by a corresponding increase in local tax revenue. Moreover, because of language barriers, the children of immigrants often cost significantly more to educate than those of natives. Most news coverage of the issue discusses how to meet the needs of these children, but fails to point out that federal immigration policy created the problem in the first place.

Despite the clear implications mass immigration has for the future of American society, many boosters still argue that today's immigration is very much like that of 1910. No doubt, there are similarities, but the differences are profound and striking to even the casual observer. America is a fundamentally different place than it was 100 years ago, and today's immigration is also very different.

Lack of Assimilation

As far as assimilation is concerned, numbers matter at least as much as percentages. For example, a quarter of a million immigrants in a metropolitan area are enough to create linguistic isolation: neighborhoods where immigrants can live and work without ever learning much English. Large numbers also create politically influential ethnic organizations whose leaders often adhere to an anti-assimilation multicultural ideology. Whether the immigrants in question represent 10 percent or 30 percent of a city's population is not so important; it's the raw numbers that count, and the numbers are already well over twice what they were in 1910.

In one sense, today's immigrants are more diverse than ever before, in that significant numbers arrive from all continents and races. But in a more important sense, today's immigration wave is considerably less diverse than those of the past, because Spanish speakers dominate in a way no other group ever did before. While German speakers accounted for a little over a quarter of all immigrants in the late 1800s and Italians for about one-fifth in the first decades of the 1900s, such concentrations were transitory. In contrast, the domination of immigrants from Latin America has grown steadily. In 1970, 19 percent of the foreign-born were from Latin America; by 2000, it was more than half. One ethnolinguistic group can now predominate in schools, neighborhoods, entire metropolitan areas, and even whole states.

One institution that helped immigrants and their children acquire an American identity in the past was public education. Schools brought children from different immigrant backgrounds into contact with natives and helped to forge a common American culture. But today, basic demographics makes this much more difficult. Unlike in the past, immigrants now have many more children on average than natives, which means kids from immigrant families very quickly predominate in public schools. For example, although about a quarter of California's total population is foreign-born, half of the school-age population is from immigrant families. In many districts in high-immigration states, immigrant families now account for more than 80 percent of school kids.

Of course, neighborhood schools in 1910 saw heavy immigrant concentrations. But because of the large differences in fertility rates, immigration today creates many more districts in which the cultural norms are set by children from immigrant families, who have relatively little contact with their counterparts from native families.

Multiculturalism

There is, of course, another problem with expecting public schools to play the role they did in the past of assimilating immigrants: Schools don't want to. A very significant share of the U.S. elite has embraced the anti-assimilation ethos, which regards America as a collection of peoples, each with its own distinct culture, which vie for political power as groups. America's educational establishment has embraced this multicultural vision. This is why history textbooks look as they do, and why bilingual education remains widely popular among educators. This trend shows no signs of abating; in fact, the growing number of immigrants only feeds the multiculturalist perspective. Immigration provides further justification for it by creating an ever larger aggrieved class, whose cultures must be preserved in the face of an oppressive majority culture.

Of course, some form of assimilation does take place, even in the modern public school. While language acquisition almost certainly has slowed in recent years, most immigrants learn to speak at least some English. But assimilation is much more than learning to speak English, or driving on the right side of the road. It involves what John Fonte of the Hudson Institute calls "patriotic assimilation," the belief that American history is one's own history. A century ago it meant that immigrants and their children came to see America's past as something "we" did, not something "they"— white people of European ancestry—did. To the extent that immigrants are assimilating they are doing so, in many cases, as "multicultural" Americans.

Some conservatives, and even some liberals, have a different conception of assimilation, but it is not at all clear that those who wish to see a more robust love of country inculcated in our children (immigrant or native) are winning the debate. It simply makes no sense, therefore, for a society that cannot agree on its own history or even what it means to be an American to welcome over a million newcomers each year from outside.

More Obstacles to Assimilation

Technology is another obstacle to assimilation. It is now possible to call—or even to visit—one's home country with a frequency that was inconceivable even 50 years ago. One can listen to a hometown radio station or read the local newspapers on the Internet. The costs of travel and communication are now so low that many wealthier immigrants can live in two countries at the same time, traveling back and forth with ease. In such a world, it is less likely that immigrants will develop a deep attachment to the U.S.

The American economy is also fundamentally different, with serious consequences for the assimilation process. A century ago, manufacturing, mining, and agriculture employed the vast majority of the workforce, creating plentiful work for unskilled immigrants. These jobs eventually led to solid working-class incomes for immigrants and their children. (In fact, most native-born Americans a century ago worked in the same kinds of jobs.) Though most people were poor by today's standards, most historians agree that there was not a very large economic gap between the standard of living of natives and that of immigrants; this was because, on average, immigrants were not that much less skilled than natives. Data are limited, but in terms of years of schooling or literacy, immigrants 100 years ago were roughly equal to natives.

This is no longer the case. While a number of today's immigrants are quite skilled, immigrants overall are significantly less educated than natives. As a result, when it comes to average income, poverty rates, welfare use, and other measures of economic well-being, today's immigrants are much worse off than natives. Unlike that of 1910, today's U.S. economy offers very limited opportunity for those with little education, and this creates a very sizable gap between the two groups.

Another important change since 1910 is the profound expansion in the size and scope of government. Spending on everything from education to infrastructure maintenance is many times greater than it was back then. With federal, state, and local government now eating up roughly one-third of GDP [gross domestic product], the average individual must be able to pay a good deal in taxes to cover his use of public services. In practice, the middle and upper classes pay most of the taxes; the poor, immigrant or native, generally consume significantly more in public services than they pay in taxes.

This means that the arrival of large numbers of relatively poor immigrants has a significant negative effect on public coffers in a way that was not the case in the past. In 1997 the National Academy of Sciences estimated that immigrant households consumed between $11 and $20 billion more in public services than they were paying in taxes each year. (Other estimates have found this deficit to be even higher.) A smaller government may well be desirable, but it is politically inconceivable that we would ever return to the situation of 100 years ago, when government accounted for a tiny fraction of the economy. Thus, continually allowing in large numbers of unskilled immigrants has very negative implications for taxpayers.

Immigration Must Be Curbed

The situation of today's immigrants is, then, dramatically different from what it was at the turn of the last century. But even if one ignores all these differences, one undeniable fact remains: The last great wave of immigration was stopped, as an act of government policy. World War I, followed by restrictive legislation in the early 1920s, dramatically reduced immigration to about a quarter of what it had been in previous decades. This immigration pause played a critically important role in turning yesterday's immigrants into Americans. So if the past is to be our guide, then we should significantly reduce immigration numbers.

If we don't, the assimilation problem will only get worse. We know from experience that it is often the children of immigrants who have the greatest difficulty identifying with America. While their parents at least know how good they have it, the children tend to compare their situation to that of other Americans, instead of that in their parents' homeland. Unless the gap between themselves and other Americans has been closed in just one generation, something few groups have been able to accomplish, this can be a source of real discontent. Moreover, it is children born in the U.S. to immigrant parents who often feel caught between two worlds and struggle with their identity.

What we should do is call a halt to the current heedless increase in annual immigration, and reduce the numbers to something like their historical average of 300,000 a year. In the mid 1990s, the bipartisan immigration-reform panel headed by the late Barbara Jordan suggested limiting family immigration to the spouses and minor children of U.S. citizens and legal non-citizens, and to the parents of citizens. However, we should probably eliminate the preferences for the spouses and minor children of non-citizens, since these provisions apply to family members acquired after the alien has received a green card but before he has become a citizen. If we also eliminated the parents of U.S. citizens as a category, family immigration would fall to less than half what it is today. The Jordan panel also wisely suggested eliminating the visa lottery and tightening up the requirements for employment and humanitarian-based immigration.

These changes would, taken together, reduce legal immigration to roughly 300,000 annually. Only if we get the numbers down to this reasonable level can we begin the long process of assimilating the huge number of immigrants and their children who are already here.

"Why shouldn't a person be free to cross a border, whether in search of work . . . or simply because he wants to?"

Strict Limits Should Not Be Imposed on Immigration

Jacob G. Hornberger

In the following viewpoint Jacob G. Hornberger argues that America was founded on the principle of freedom, and that immigration restrictions are a violation of that principle. People should be free to travel wherever they wish, he maintains. In Hornberger's opinion, immigrants will not destroy American culture, smuggle in drugs, or take jobs away from Americans. He believes that the United States should keep its borders open to whoever wishes to enter. Hornberger is founder and president of the Future of Freedom Foundation and coauthor of *The Case for Free Trade and Open Immigration.*

As you read, consider the following questions:
1. When did the founding fathers' concept of freedom begin to deteriorate, as argued by the author?
2. In Hornberger's opinion, in addition to affecting foreigners, how do immigration controls impact the freedom of the American people?
3. According to the author, how do immigrants positively impact America's job market?

In times of crisis, it is sometimes wise and constructive for people to return to first principles and to reexamine where we started as a nation, the road we've traveled, where we are today, and the direction in which we're headed. Such a reevaluation can help determine whether a nation has deviated from its original principles and, if so, whether a restoration of those principles would be in order.

It is impossible to overstate the unusual nature of American society from the time of its founding to the early part of the twentieth century. Imagine: no Social Security, Medicare, Medicaid, income tax, welfare, systems of public (i.e., government) schooling, occupational licensure, standing armies, foreign aid, foreign interventions, or foreign wars. Perhaps most unusual of all, there were virtually no federal controls on immigration into the United States.

With the tragic and costly exception of slavery, the bedrock principle underlying American society was that people should be free to live their lives any way they chose, as long as their conduct was peaceful. That is what it once meant to be free. That is what it once meant to be an American. That was the freedom that our ancestors celebrated each Fourth of July.

Beginning in the early part of the twentieth century, however, our founders' concept of freedom was gradually abandoned in favor of a totally different concept—one that defined freedom in terms of the government's taking care of people, both domestically and internationally, together with the unlimited power to tax the citizenry to pay for that service.

Whatever might be said about the relative merits of the welfare state and the regulated society, their adoption effected a revolutionary transformation in the way that the American people viewed their freedom and the role of government in their lives. Moreover, the welfare-state revolution has had enormous consequences on the daily lives of the American people.

Open and Free Immigration

Let's examine the issue of immigration, which provides a good model for comparing our ancestors' vision of freedom with what guides the American people today.

In economic terms, the concept of freedom to which the founders subscribed entailed the right to sustain one's life through labor by pursuing any occupation or business without government permission or interference. It also meant freely entering into mutually beneficial exchanges with others anywhere in the world, accumulating unlimited amounts of wealth arising from those endeavors, and freely deciding the disposition of that wealth.

The moral question is: Why shouldn't a person be free to cross a border, whether in search of work to sustain his life, to open a business, to tour, or simply because he wants to? Or to put it another way, under what moral authority does any government interfere with the exercise of these rights?

We Americans often take for granted the idea of open borders within the United States, but it is such an important gift from our founders that it deserves thoughtful reflection. Think about it: Hundreds of millions of people are free to travel on the highways through all states without ever being stopped by a border guard. It is a way of life that would have shocked most people throughout history and that still surprises many foreigners who experience it for the first time.

Most Americans like the concept of open borders within the United States, but what distinguished our ancestors is that they believed that the principles of freedom were applicable not just domestically but universally. That implied open borders not only for people traveling inside the United States but also for people traveling or moving to the United States.

One important result of this highly unusual philosophy of freedom was that through most of the nineteenth century, people all over the world, especially those who were suffering political tyranny or economic privation, always knew that there was a place they could go if they could succeed in escaping their circumstances.

Immoral Results of Restrictions

The American abandonment of open immigration in the twentieth century has had negative consequences, both morally and economically. Let's consider some examples.

Prior to and during World War II, U.S. government officials intentionally used immigration controls to prevent

German Jews from escaping the horrors of Nazi Germany by coming to America. Many of us are familiar with the infamous "voyage of the damned," in which a German ship was prohibited from landing in Miami became it carried Jewish refugees.

But how many people know that U.S. officials used immigration controls to keep German Jews and eastern European Jews from coming to the United States even after the existence of the concentration camps became well known? Indeed, how many Americans know about the one million anticommunist Russians whom U.S. and British officials forcibly repatriated to the Soviet Union at the end of World War II, knowing that death or the gulag awaited them?

Immigrants and Welfare

Contrary to stereotypes, there is no evidence that immigrants come to this country to receive welfare. Indeed, most studies show that immigrants actually use welfare at lower rates than do native-born Americans. For example, a study of welfare recipients in New York City found that only 7.7% of immigrants were receiving welfare compared to 13.3% for the population as a whole. Likewise, a nationwide study by the U.S. Bureau of Labor Statistics found that 12.8% of immigrants were receiving welfare benefits, compared to 13.9% of the general population. Some recent studies indicate that the rate of welfare usage may now be equalizing between immigrants and native-born Americans, but, clearly, most immigrants are not on welfare.

Michael Tanner, 1995. www.lp.org.

Ancient history, you say? Consider one of the most morally reprehensible policies in the history of our nation: the forcible repatriation of Cuban refugees into communist tyranny, a practice that has been going on for many years and continues to this day.

Let me restate this for emphasis: Under the pretext of enforcing immigration laws, our government—the U.S. government—the same government that sent tens of thousands of American GIs [soldiers] to their deaths in foreign wars supposedly to resist communism, is now forcibly returning people to communism. . . . How can this conduct be reconciled with the fundamental principles of freedom and morality on which our nation was founded?

It's also important to note that immigration controls affect not only foreigners but also the freedom of the American people, especially such fundamental rights as freedom of association, freedom of contract, and privacy. We should keep in mind [economist and philosopher] Ludwig von Mises' observation that one government intervention inevitably produces perverse consequences that then lead to an ever-increasing array of new interventions. The government began with immigration quotas. Over time, we have seen the growth of an enormous government bureaucracy (the INS [Immigration and Naturalization Service] and Border Patrol) that harasses, abuses, and terrorizes large segments of the population.

We have seen the establishment of Border Patrol passport checkpoints on highways and airports inside the United States (north of the border), which inevitably discriminate against people on the basis of skin color. We have seen the criminalization of such things as transporting, housing, and hiring undocumented workers, followed by arbitary detentions on highways as well as raids on American farms and restaurants.

We have seen the construction of a fortified wall in California. This wall, built soon after the fall of the ugliest wall in history [the Berlin Wall], has resulted in the deaths of immigrants entering the country through the harsh Arizona desert.

Objections and Answers

Would [founding fathers George] Washington, [Thomas] Jefferson, or [James] Madison have constructed such a wall? We have come a long way from the vision of freedom set forth by our Founding Fathers.

Let's consider some of the common objections to open immigration.

1. Open immigration will pollute America's culture. Which culture is that? Boston? New York? Savannah? New Orleans? Denver? Los Angeles? I grew up on the Mexican border (on the Texas side). My culture was eating enchiladas and tacos, listening to both Mexican and American music, and speaking Tex-Mex (a combination of English and Span-

ish). America's culture has always been one of liberty—one in which people are free to pursue any culture they want.

2. Immigrants will take jobs away from Americans. Immigrants displace workers in certain sectors, but the displaced workers benefit through the acquisition of higher-paying jobs in other sectors that expand because of the influx of immigrants. It is not a coincidence that, historically, our standard of living has soared when borders have been open. Keep in mind also that traditionally immigrants are among the hardest working and most energetic people in a society, which brings positive vitality and energy.

3. Immigrants will go on welfare. Maybe we ought to reexamine whether it was a good idea to abandon the principles of our ancestors in that respect as well. What would be wrong with abolishing welfare for everyone, including Americans, along with the enormous taxation required to fund it? But if Americans are addicted to the government dole, there is no reason that the same thing has to happen to immigrants. Therefore, the answer to the welfare issue is not to control immigration but rather to deny immigrants the right to go on the government dole. In such a case, however, wouldn't it be fair to exempt them from the taxes used to fund the U.S. welfare state?

4. Immigrants will bring in drugs. Lots of people bring in drugs, including Americans returning from overseas trips. Not even the harshest police state would ever alter that fact. Why not legalize drugs and make the state leave drug users alone?

5. There will be too many people. Who decides the ideal number? A government board of central planners, just like in China? Wouldn't reliance on the free market to make such a determination be more consistent with our founding principles? Immigrants go where the opportunities abound and avoid areas where they don't, just as Americans do.

6. Open immigration will permit terrorists to enter our country. The only permanent solution to terrorism against the United States is to address the flaws in U.S. foreign policy, which is the breeding ground for terrorism against our country. No immigration controls in the world, not even a rebuilt Berlin Wall around the United States, will succeed in

preventing the entry of people who are bound and determined to kill Americans.

More than 200 years ago, ordinary people brought into existence the most unusual society in history. It was a society based on the fundamental moral principle that people everywhere are endowed with certain inherent rights that no government can legitimately take away.

Somewhere along the way, Americans abandoned that concept of freedom, especially in their attachment to such programs and policies as Social Security, Medicare, Medicaid, income taxation, economic regulation, public schooling, the war on drugs, the war on poverty, the war on wealth, immigration controls, foreign aid, foreign intervention, and foreign wars—none of which our founders had ever dreamed of.

The current crisis provides us with an opportunity to reexamine our founding principles, why succeeding generations of Americans abandoned them, the consequences of that abandonment, and whether it would be wise to restore the founders' moral and philosophical principles of freedom. A good place to start such a reexamination would be immigration.

"Solid and conclusive reforms in American primary and secondary education remain elusive."

America's Education System Must Be Improved

Koret Task Force on K–12 Education

The following viewpoint is excerpted from a report by the Koret Task Force on K–12 Education, which reviewed the state of America's education system in 2003. According to the task force, while the necessity of significant educational reforms was recognized in 1983, the nation has made little progress toward achieving these reforms. America's educational achievements are poor compared with other countries', states the task force. It recommends a major transformation of the system, based on the principles of accountability, choice, and transparency. The Koret Task Force is composed of eleven nationally known scholars and was sponsored by the Koret Foundation, an organization dedicated to educational reform and youth development.

As you read, consider the following questions:
1. According to the task force, what type of coping and compensating mechanisms have been making up for America's poor educational system?
2. What does transparency in education mean, as explained by the authors?
3. What will be the result of rekindling Americans' confidence in public education, according to the task force?

Twenty years ago [in 1983], the National Commission on Excellence in Education (Excellence Commission) delivered a thunderbolt in the form of a report called *A Nation at Risk*. With the hindsight that two decades can provide, it is clear that this report awakened millions of Americans to a national crisis in primary and secondary education. *A Nation at Risk* bluntly and forcefully pinpointed the problems facing our public schools and insisted that their solution would require a new commitment to education quality, on the part of school administrators, teachers, parents, and students. Though the Excellence Commission did not consider some of the far-reaching reforms that would later become an important part of the national discourse, it did help set the stage for such reforms by pointing to worrisome signs of weakness and decay in our school system.

That system did not suddenly crash in the early eighties. The declines, shortcomings, and inadequacies so starkly set forth in *A Nation at Risk* had been accumulating for many years. But until the Excellence Commission documented and framed them as grave problems in urgent need of attention, many Americans—especially those within the field of education—had supposed that the schools were doing an adequate job and that, whatever its shortcomings, the system was sufficient to meet the country's needs.

The Excellence Commission called an abrupt halt to this smug contentment. It admonished the nation in forceful, martial language that America faced a momentous problem, one that threatened its national security, and its economic vitality. Not since the late fifties, when Sputnik startled the nation with the possibility that the Soviet Union was surpassing us in science and mathematics, had there been such alarm over the academic weakness of U.S. schools.[1]

A Lack of Progress

Within a few years after Sputnik, the sense of urgency had faded and the focus of reform had turned away from academic performance. Well-intended efforts to address racial

1. In 1957 the Soviet Union launched Sputnik I, the first artificial satellite to be launched into orbit.

segregation, meet the needs of handicapped youngsters, compensate for disadvantage, and provide bilingual schooling for immigrants eclipsed concern about student achievement. They also produced much red tape, litigiousness, and contentious battles over means and ends. Teacher organizations, at the same time, asserted their right to bargain collectively and to strike, which brought them unprecedented power over schools and school systems, even as other interest groups and bureaucratic rigidities made it ever harder to change public education. In other words, the Sputnik-inspired commitment to improving the education system had clearly lost priority—as had student achievement. SAT [Scholastic Achievement Test] scores peaked in 1964 and declined thereafter, reaching their nadir about the time *A Nation at Risk* was unleashed.

Yet twenty years following the alarm sounded by *A Nation at Risk*, the commitment has not faded. Thanks to the report's eloquence and official standing in Washington, D.C., it reinforced and dramatized concerns expressed by a simultaneous outpouring of other reports, studies, and manifestos all pointing to the fact that American students were not learning enough and U.S. schools were not performing well enough to meet international competition. . . . But while its reverberations are still being felt, solid and conclusive reforms in American primary and secondary education remain elusive. . . .

Findings of the Koret Task Force

The members of this task force have studied American education for many years. We come from several disciplines and have different interests. But we come together in unanimous support of the ten findings and three major recommendations that follow. These encompass the most important lessons we have learned about American K–12 education over the two decades since *A Nation at Risk*.

1. *U.S. education outcomes, measured in many ways, show little improvement since 1970.* The trends that alarmed the Excellence Commission have not been reversed. Though small gains can be seen in some areas (especially math), they amount to no more than a return to the achievement levels of thirty years ago. And while the United States runs in

place, other nations are overtaking us. In the past, we could always boast that America educates a larger proportion of its school-age children than other lands, but this is no longer true. Many countries now match and exceed us in years of school attained by their youth, and they are surpassing us as well in what is actually learned during those years.

2. *The U.S. economy has fared well during the past two decades not because of the strong performance of its K–12 system, but because of a host of coping and compensating mechanisms.* These include an endlessly forgiving (and generously remediating) higher education system; the presence within the United States of most of the world's top universities; huge efforts at research and development (leading, for example, to notable productivity gains that owe little to workers' skills); a hardworking populace and an adaptable immigration policy; a society that encourages second chances and invites new ideas; and the world's largest and best-functioning free market economy. Yet even as we have racked up successes in economic and foreign policy domains, we have also seen unmistakable evidence of civic erosion, cultural decline, and moral wavering.

3. *We've made progress in narrowing resource gaps between schools, communities, states, and groups, but the achievement gaps that vex us remain nearly as wide as ever.* This is because the problems that *A Nation at Risk* highlighted particularly affect schools that serve disadvantaged children, and these problems have not been successfully addressed. Minority youngsters are far less apt to complete school and college, and their average academic performance is markedly lower. On some measures, minority twelfth-graders score about the same as white eighth-graders, who themselves are not scoring well. The bottom line: America's primary-secondary education system not only remains mediocre, but its failure to reform also has strikingly inequitable consequences for poor and minority children. . . .

4. *Higher-quality teachers are key to improving our schools, but the proper gauge to measure that quality has nothing to do with paper credentials or more resources and everything to do with classroom effectiveness.* Across-the-board raises for all teachers, good and bad alike, do not strengthen pupil learning. And

stricter regulation of teacher preparation and accreditation only creates shortages and bottlenecks that reduce the supply of capable new instructors for U.S. schools.

5. *Bold reform attempts have been implemented in limited and piece-meal fashion, despite their potential to improve student learning.* It has been demonstrated in several states that "accountability," or standards-based, reform, when done persistently and carefully, can boost achievement, especially among minority and disadvantaged youngsters. And "choice-based" reform has shown promise and is in great demand, as witnessed by the growth of the charter school movement, the rise in home schooling, and parental and community support for scholarship and voucher programs.

Racial Segregation in Education

Many children—African American and white—are still attending virtually one-race schools. Segregation has found its way back—if, indeed, it ever left some schools.

To be sure, today's racial separation is not sanctioned by law. But in terms of racial isolation, the effect is much the same, and with the same consequences. . . . We are still trying to bring up to speed predominantly black schools—often located in poverty-stricken communities—by spending money on compensatory programs and other catch-up improvements to increase educational opportunities for minority students.

Colbert I. King, *Liberal Opinion Week*, March 8, 2004.

6. *Standards-based reform has not achieved its full potential. Though promising, it is hard to get right.* States find it difficult to gain consensus on a coherent set of substantial and ambitious academic standards, to align their tests with those standards, and to get strong accountability systems working. Standards and tests are essential for parents and policy makers to identify faltering schools and gauge the effectiveness of different programs, but they do not themselves solve the problems that they illumine. Moreover, the steps taken so far in the name of accountability fall, for the most part, only upon children, not on the adults in the system. . . .

7. *Americans need better, more timely information about student performance, not only at the national and international lev-*

els, but also for individual schools, pupils, and teachers. We need more and clearer data about what schools do, where they spend their money, and what results they're producing. Currently, the only audits of the system's performance are conducted by those running the system or by organizations that depend upon them for future business, including colleges of education and testing firms. As the country has recently and painfully observed in the business world, such audits are simply unsatisfactory from the standpoint of the system's stakeholders and clients.

8. *We need a thoroughgoing reform of elementary and middle schooling.* Though our high schools require attention, preschool and K–8 education are far from what they need to be. These are the years when children gain fundamental knowledge about their country and their world, about science and literature, about art and civics. This calls for close attention to K–8 curricula as well as to the curricular aspects of prekindergarten education and for purposeful steps to help prepare all children to succeed in kindergarten and beyond.

Our Recommendations

In the years since *A Nation at Risk*, the incremental changes that passed for reform have not improved school performance or student achievement. We conclude that fundamental changes are needed in the incentive structures and power relationships of schooling itself. Those changes are anchored to three core principles: *accountability, choice, and transparency.*

By *accountability*, we mean that every school or education provider—at least every one that accepts public dollars—subscribes to a coherent set of rigorous, statewide academic standards, statewide assessments of student and school performance, and statewide systems of incentives and interventions tied to academic results in relation to those standards. . . .

By *choice* we mean that parental decisions rather than bureaucratic regulation should drive the education enterprise. Open competition among ideas and methods, with people free to abandon weak schools for stronger ones, is the surest way to make major progress. The concept that underlies charter school—freedom of operation in return for evidence of satisfactory results—makes sense at every level of education. It is the central doctrine of modern management: Operators of a production unit enjoy sweeping autonomy to run their unit as they think best but are strictly held to account for the bottom line. In education, that bottom line is denominated primarily in terms of student learning and parental satisfaction. The education system's clients must be free to select other providers that teach their children more effectively and in accord with family and community priorities as well as core American values. . . .

By *transparency* we mean that those who seek complete information about a school or school system (excluding personal information about individuals) should readily be able to get it. This information should be provided in forms and formats that enable users to easily compare one school, system, or state with another. . . .

Reinvigorating the System

Accountability, choice, and transparency are the essential trinity of principles by which to reconstruct America's schools. Each must be in place for the others to work. In combination, they transform the education system's priorities, power relationships, and incentive structures. . . .

Taken together, the result of these three will be a reinvigorated yet very different public education system, a new constitutional arrangement with power distributed where it belongs, checks and balances among those who wield that power, and incentives that pull toward—rather than away from—achievement, productivity, freedom, and accountability.

This new system will rekindle Americans' confidence in public education and this should lead to a greater public willingness—once people understand how and why additional resources will make a difference—to invest more in education. Such new investments, in turn, could lead to even greater gains, such as abler people entering and staying in the teaching field; better preschooling; better technology and textbooks; and better performance in the classroom.

The rebirth of this confidence, however, requires the radical overhaul we have outlined here.

> "*American education is better today than it was in 1983. And we are on the verge of making it much better.*"

America's Education System Has Improved

James B. Hunt Jr.

In 2003 the Koret Task Force on K–12 Education released a report reviewing the state of America's education system, concluding that it was in jeopardy and that drastic changes needed to be made to improve it. In the following viewpoint James B. Hunt Jr. disagrees. In his opinion, there have already been tremendous improvements made to America's education system in the past twenty years. He argues that standards have been raised significantly, teacher quality has increased, and research about brain development has greatly helped in developing effective teaching methods. Hunt is chairman of the board at the James B. Hunt Jr. Institute for Educational Leadership and Policy at the University of North Carolina. He is also the former governor of North Carolina.

As you read, consider the following questions:

1. According to the author, why was the 1983 report *A Nation at Risk* "like a meteor hitting the ocean"?
2. How many states now lack standards, according to Hunt?
3. How does knowledge about children's brain development help educators, as explained by the author?

James B. Hunt Jr., "Unrecognized Progress," *Education Next*, vol. 3, Spring 2003, pp. 24–27. Copyright © 2003 by *Education Next*. Reproduced by permission.

The Koret Task Force does a valuable service for American education.[1] Its recommendations are largely on target as we stick with the task of improving our schools and move toward the goal of "leaving no child behind." But I see the events of the past 20 years in a different light. Our educators, students, parents, and policymakers deserve much more credit for what has been accomplished. While improvement has come in fits and starts—and detoured into a number of deadends—American education is better today than it was in 1983. And we are on the verge of making it much better.

I was governor of North Carolina in 1983 when the National Commission on Excellence in Education released *A Nation at Risk*.[2] Against heavy opposition, I had pushed hard to begin statewide testing of our public school students. Our early assessments had revealed major deficiencies. *Risk* showed that this was a nationwide phenomenon. Many policymakers sensed that the report would provide a major boost to our efforts to bring about serious change in education. . . .

The release of *Risk* acted like a meteor hitting the ocean, creating tidal waves of reform everywhere. Another report of the mid-1980s, the Carnegie Corporation's *A Nation Prepared*, sparked a long focus on excellence in teaching in an effort to define what Tom Kean, former governor of New Jersey, termed "what accomplished teachers need to know and be able to do." Nearly every leader of the NGA [National Governors Association], Republicans and Democrats alike, made education, standards, and economic competitiveness a theme of his chairmanship. Then, in 1989, the governors and President George H.W. Bush held the nation's first education summit in Charlottesville, Virginia, and formulated national education goals for America.

Three major developments of the past 20 years are now bearing fruit: 1) the creation of standards and accountability; 2) research on how the brain develops in early childhood and

---

1. In 2003 the Koret Task Force released a report reviewing the status of American education, and making suggestions for improvement. According to the report, education has not improved significantly in the past twenty years.   2. This 1983 report warned that the American education system was in crisis.

its implications for pre-K education and child care; and 3) an emerging focus on the single biggest factor in student achievement—teacher quality.

Standards and Accountability

While the Koret report finds that "standards-based reforms . . . though promising . . . are hard to get right," the truth is that most states have been working hard to "get it right" and have met with good success. Groups like Achieve, the Business Roundtable, ECS [Education Commissioner of the States] and the recent summits led by IBM CEO [chief executive officer] Louis Gerstner have had a real impact. Most of the nation's governors have gotten the message: if you aren't pushing hard to set high standards and making considerable progress toward achieving them, your state will not be "the place" for business to locate and jobs to be created.

Only a handful of states now lack standards. Most need better standards than they have, but they have made a good start. In 1983 only a handful of states had *any* standards, and we were measuring progress in education almost solely by the increase in spending rather than achievement.

It is easy to criticize the work of states and school districts on standards, but dedicated teachers, principals, superintendents, and curriculum experts have spent untold hours trying to build their systems. They deserve our commendation. Some were especially bold. Virginia and Massachusetts can attest to the agony involved in setting high standards and, as a result, having many students fail the exams. But they can also attest to the value of sticking with this venture—providing greater support to students and teachers and thus seeing test scores climb dramatically. Others are emulating them.

Any fair assessment of the events of the two decades since *Risk* must conclude that we are well on our way to high and rigorous standards and accountability. We should be proud of that progress and committed to do a lot better.

Ready to Learn

The Koret report hardly mentions one of the most important developments since *Risk:* science's remarkable progress in understanding how a child's brain develops in the earliest years and the ensuing efforts to provide the early child care and education necessary for school readiness.

We now know that all children are born with about the same number of brain cells, billions of them. But the capacity for intelligence is largely set early in the child's life, when those brain cells are connected up. These connections are formed largely from stimulation—hearing sounds, seeing colors, feeling things, responding to love and care.

No Child Left Behind

In January 2001, only 11 states were in full compliance with previous Federal education accountability standards. So, President [George W.] Bush called for significant reforms to K–12 education through No Child Left Behind to set high standards and produce real results for every child in America. President Bush signed into law the No Child Left Behind Act to help the youngest Americans receive a quality education and learn the basic skills they need to succeed in the future. No Child Left Behind is providing increased funding for education, closing the achievement gap that exists between students of different socio-economic backgrounds, and providing more information and better options for parents.

All skills begin with the basics of reading and math, which should be learned in the early grades in America's schools. Yet for too long and for too many children, those skills were never mastered. With the bipartisan No Child Left Behind Act, America is making progress toward educational excellence for every child.

Education: The Promise of America, September 26, 2004. www.whitehouse.gov.

We also know a great deal now about *what* is happening *when* in a child's development. This enables educators to help young, inexperienced parents know what to look for and how to be most helpful to their child's development.

This knowledge is part of the research base that has propelled quality child care and education to the forefront as a strategy for educational success. Roughly half of the "achievement gap" is already present when poor, minority children enter the schoolhouse door. The inescapable conclusion is that we must help these children get a better start early in life.

Teacher Quality

The Koret report misses the mark most seriously with regard to teaching. It states, "Higher quality teachers are key to improving our schools, but the proper gauge to measure that quality has nothing to do with paper credentials." It goes on to say that the only true gauge of teacher quality is "classroom effectiveness." Of course that is the best measure. But how do we get teachers who are effective in boosting student achievement? How do we improve their knowledge and skills? How do we keep them in the classroom? Fortunately, lots of people have been working on answers to those questions.

In 1996 the National Commission on Teaching and America's Future challenged the nation to provide every child with what should be his or her educational birthright: "access to competent, caring, qualified teaching in schools organized for success." It urged the nation to get serious about teacher standards, reinvent teacher preparation and professional development, put qualified teachers in every classroom, encourage and reward teacher knowledge and skill, and create schools organized for student and teacher success. Twenty states joined together as partners to implement the recommendations, while others have taken some action.

Major business groups have taken up the quest for better teaching and are pushing for higher standards for teachers, better preparation and professional development, and higher pay linked to performance. They also urged the creation of a corps of "master" teachers certified by the National Board for Professional Teaching Standards. Today there are nearly 24,000 national board-certified teachers found in all 50 states. They meet rigorous standards. They receive extra compensation in many states and districts—$6,000 per year more in Mississippi and $7,500 more in South Carolina. They are superb teachers for their students and mentors and role models to fellow teachers.

"A personal account . . . will allow you to earn some money, it grows over time, and if you pass away early, it's an asset you can pass on."

Diverting Money into Private Accounts Would Strengthen Social Security

George W. Bush

The following viewpoint is excerpted from a speech by George W. Bush. He argues that America's Social Security system is in crisis and will eventually be unable to provide for the retirement needs of elderly Americans. Under the current system there are no individual accounts; instead tax receipts from current workers are used to pay current benefits to retirees. Bush advocates private accounts as a way to improve this system. In Bush's opinion, private accounts are superior to the current system because they have greater yields and will become assets that individuals can pass on to their families. He points out that the viability of this idea has been proven through the success of a similar savings plan that federal employees currently use. Bush is the former governor of Texas and the forty-third president of the United States.

As you read, consider the following questions:

1. According to the author, in the 1950s how many workers were there for every Social Security beneficiary?
2. What will the Social Security deficit be in the 2030s, as argued by Bush?
3. As explained by the author, what currently happens when two family members are receiving Social Security and one dies?

George W. Bush, speech at Albuquerque, New Mexico, March 22, 2005.

Let me start off on Social Security by telling you I believe the President's jobs and I believe senators' jobs are to confront problems, not to pass them on to future Presidents and future Congresses. I believe that is why we get elected in the first place.

A Broken System

We have a problem in Social Security. [U.S. president] Franklin Roosevelt did a good thing when he created the Social Security system. And it has worked for a lot of folks. Social Security has provided an important safety net for many, many senior citizens. But what I want to explain to you—and I think others will here, as well—is that times have changed. The math has changed on Social Security. In other words, let me put it to you this way—there's a lot of people getting ready to retire called baby boomers. I'm one. I was born in 1946. My retirement—I reach retirement age in 2008. It turns out to be a convenient moment. A lot of people like me . . . are starting to retire in 2008. There is a bulge, baby boomer bulge, a lot of us.

Interestingly enough, we are now living longer than previous generations. When Social Security was first started, life expectancy was a heck of a lot lower than it is today. Plus, many politicians in previous years ran for office saying, vote for me, I will increase your Social Security benefits. In other words, I'll increase the promises. So my generation has been promised more benefits than the previous generation. A lot of us, living longer, getting paid more money, with fewer people paying into the system. That's the other side of the equation. . . .

In the 1950s there were 16 workers for every beneficiary. In other words, the load was pretty light. Today it's 3.3 to 1 workers—in other words, 3.3 workers to every beneficiary. You got a lot of us living longer, getting greater benefits, with fewer people paying the load, see. And pretty soon it's going to be 2 to 1. And so you can imagine, longer life with greater beneficiaries—in other words, the obligations are increasing quite dramatically with fewer people carrying the load. And guess who gets to carry the load. The young workers.

And the fundamental question—this isn't an issue, frankly,

about the older generation. You're going to get your check. You're in good shape. It's really an issue of whether or not this government and this country understands the burden we're going to place on younger Americans coming up. That's what the issue is all about. And here is the burden. This is a pay-as-you-go system: money goes in and it goes out. Somebody probably thinks, well, there's a trust—in other words, we're taking your money and we'll hold it for you, and then when you retire we give it back to you. That's not how it works. It's pay-as-you-go; the money comes in and we go ahead and pay. We pay for a lot of things other than Social Security. Retirement checks are sent out, and if there's money left over, it goes to fund all aspects of government. And what is left behind is a piece of paper, an IOU.

More Money Going Out than Coming In

In 2018, because the math has changed, more money will be going out than coming in for Social Security. People will be paying payroll taxes, but because baby boomers like me are retired and we're living longer and we're getting bigger benefits than the previous generation, the system turns into the red. And every year thereafter, if we don't do anything, it gets worse and worse and worse.

To give you a sense of how big a problem it will be for a younger generation and younger workers, in 2027 we'll be $200 billion in the hole. That's $200 billion more than coming in for payroll taxes. It will be bigger in 2028, 2029, and in the 2030s it gets up to $300 billion. So you're getting a sense of the magnitude of the problem. Unlike the old days, when 16 workers would pay into the system for every beneficiary, it was a manageable issue, the math worked. Math doesn't work now.

And that's why I went in front of the Congress and said, folks, we got to do something now before it's too late. The experts will tell you the longer we wait, the harder it is to get the problem solved. And so that's why I'm traveling the country I'm saying two things right off the bat: One, we have got a serious problem for the younger generation. And two, if you're getting your check, if you're born prior to 1950, the government is going to keep its promise to you, nothing changes.

Now, at my State of the Union, I said to the Congress, I'm willing to listen to any good idea. I said, bring your ideas forward, please. In order to solve this problem, it's not going to be a Republican idea or a Democrat idea, it's going to be an American idea brought forth by both either Republicans or Democrats, or both. That's what needs to be done on this issue. That's what we got to do to fix it permanently. . . .

Ramirez. © 2004 by Copley News Service. Reproduced by permission.

If we're going to fix it, let's fix it forever, is what I'm saying to members of Congress. Let's come to the table—all ideas are on the table—and let's get this problem solved once and for all.

Private Accounts

Now, I've got an idea that I think the American people ought to seriously consider, and that is younger workers ought to be allowed to set aside some of their own money in a personal savings account as a part of the Social Security system—not the way to fix the system, it's going to require other matters to fix the system, but as a way to make the system better for the individual worker.

Let me tell you why I like the idea. . . . First, I like voluntary ideas. In other words, if you so choose, you should have the option. The government is not going to say, you must do this, but if this is an appealing idea for you, then you ought to be allowed to take some of your own money and set it aside in a personal savings account that you own yourself.

Secondly, the rate of return in a conservative mix—and notice I say, conservative mix—of bonds and stocks is greater than that which the government earns with your money. And that rate of return, the bigger rate of return is important, because over time, if you hold it, your money grows, see. And it's that growth, that compounding rate of interest, that will make the system better for the individual worker.

Let me just give you an idea. If you're earning $35,000 over your lifetime, and say, the system says you can take a third of your payroll taxes and put it in a personal account and in a conservative mix of bonds and stocks, that will yield you over your lifetime when you get ready to retire—when you get ready to retire—$250,000, see. And the way the system would work is that $250,000 is yours; you live off the interest off the $250,000 plus that which the government can afford to pay you.

Creating a Personal Asset

Now, another benefit of having your own personal account is that it's yours. It's real. It's not an IOU from one form—part of government to the other, like the current system does. It's your asset. It's something you own. And I like the idea of encouraging ownership throughout all walks of life. You can leave it to whomever you want. You see, it will help you in your retirement. You can't liquidate the plan upon retirement because it's a part of the retirement system. But your estate—you can leave it to whomever you want. You want to leave it to your daughter, fine. Leave it to [her]—you want to leave it to Colin, your son, leave it to your son. And then that person can use it for whatever he or she chooses. . . .

Thirdly, this is fair for families. The way the current system works today, if you got two—two folks working in the family, they're both contributing to Social Security, the husband or wife dies young, the spouse either gets either the survivor benefits, or his or her own Social Security check, which ever is higher, but not both. You see what I'm saying? I'm saying both contribute to the system, but if only one is living—in other words, a lot of folks die young, unfortunately, in America—it means that the spouse is only going to get the benefits of one person's contribution, not both. That doesn't seem fair to me. If somebody has worked all their life, or 30 years of their life, and dies early, it seems like that contribution ought to be worth something to the family.

And that's what a personal account will do. It will allow you to earn some money, it grows over time, and if you pass away early, it's an asset you can pass on to help your widow or your children get an education. . . .

A couple other points I want to make to you. First of all, you noticed I've been saying a conservative mix of bonds and stocks. In other words, you can't take your money and put it in a lottery. You can't take it to the track. . . . There's a way that you invest . . . that will get you a good rate of return without, obviously, risking your retirement. . . .

Part of a Permanent Solution

I speak confidently about this subject on being able to have a rational plan for people to be able to get a better rate of return, because this isn't a new idea. It's a new idea to apply it to Social Security, but it's an old idea. The Federal Employee Thrift Savings Plan allows for federal employees to do just what I'm describing to you, take some of their own money, set it aside so their money grows faster.

My attitude is pretty clear on this one. I said, if Congress thinks it's good enough for the federal employees, including themselves, sure seems good enough for the average worker in America. And so I'm talking about these ideas as a way to make the system work better for an individual worker, as a mix, as a part of an overall solution, permanent solution, because I believe all ideas ought to be on the table. And I think the American people want all ideas on the table. I think the American people expect members of both political parties to come and negotiate in good faith with all ideas on the table, in order to solve this issue permanently.

> *"Diverting money into private accounts would weaken Social Security . . . and do nothing to ensure long-term solvency."*

Diverting Money into Private Accounts Would Weaken Social Security

Douglas Holbrook

The following viewpoint is excerpted from congressional testimony given by Douglas Holbrook, vice president of the American Association of Retired Persons (AARP), an organization dedicated to advancing the interests of the elderly population. Under America's current Social Security system, tax receipts from current workers are used to pay current benefits to retirees. Holbrook argues that changing this system to create individual private accounts will weaken it and jeopardize the security of future retirees. Social Security is the only retirement plan many Americans have, maintains Holbrook, and investing this core income in private accounts is too risky. In his opinion, less drastic measures, such as increasing the wage base for Social Security, are a better way to deal with future projected shortfalls.

As you read, consider the following questions:

1. According to Holbrook, what are the four pillars of retirement security?
2. According to the author, if the wage cap for Social Security was raised to $140,000, by what percentage would Social Security's projected shortfall be lowered?
3. In what way does AARP support the use of private accounts for retirement, according to Holbrook?

Douglas Holbrook, testimony before the U.S. Senate Democratic Policy Committee, Washington, DC, January 28, 2005.

S ocial Security is crucial to the economic security of more than 47 million Americans, and making certain that it is strong for future generations is a top priority of AARP [American Association of Retired Persons].

In this age of heightened insecurity, the last thing the American people deserve is a threat to their own future financial security—and a threat to one of the most successful federal government programs in U.S. history.

Yet as we stand here today, Social Security stands in the line of fire. Steps must be taken to strengthen Social Security for the future. But there is a right way and a wrong way.

The Wrong Solution

The wrong way is to take some of the hard-earned money workers pay into Social Security and divert it into private accounts.

Diverting money into private accounts would weaken Social Security, put benefits for future retirees at risk, and do nothing to ensure long-term solvency. Private accounts are NOT a way to strengthen Social Security.

Further, the transition to a private account system would cost trillions of dollars. That would add to the federal deficit and increase the federal debt. That is not the legacy we want to leave to our children and grandchildren.

Unacceptable Risk

AARP believes there is a better way to strengthen Social Security. We are firmly committed to ensuring that the only guaranteed source of retirement security for America's families is not put at risk.

Social Security is the only guaranteed, inflation-proof, lifelong benefit that millions of workers—present and future—can count on. And we should not be talking about replacing this rock-solid core of income security with a risky gamble.

There are four pillars to retirement security and only one that is guaranteed—Social Security. The others pillars are pensions and savings; continued earnings; and health insurance.

But, less than half of working Americans have a pension plan where they work. Personal savings are at an all-time low.

The fact is, two-thirds of Americans age 65 and over get at least half of their income from Social Security. Lower wage workers and minorities depend even more heavily on Social Security for their retirement income. For one-third of beneficiaries, especially older women, Social Security is nearly their entire income—and Social Security is all that stands between them and a life of poverty. And when you consider the trends in private pensions and personal savings, we expect Social Security to be just as important for the boomers when they retire during the next several decades.

Reasonable Adjustments

We all know that Social Security faces a long-term financial problem. But, by making some reasonable adjustments today we won't have to take drastic action tomorrow.

The first thing we need to make clear is that Social Security is financially strong. The program is not in crisis. We need to remind people that even after 2042 when the trust fund is exhausted, Social Security can pay over 70 percent of current law benefits for decades. Once people understand this fact, they are much more open to options that will strengthen Social Security for the long haul.

However, it is true that the system needs long-term measures to be able to pay full benefits to boomers and future generations.

Creating private accounts funded with money diverted from Social Security is the wrong way to deal with a projected shortfall decades from now. But there is a right way. Here are two examples of what we can do:

- First, we can increase the wage base for Social Security contributions. Currently, about 85 percent of total wages nationwide are subject to Social Security payroll taxes. That figure was 90 percent for many years.

  The maximum wage subject to Social Security payments in 2005 is $90,000. Raising that cap to again cover about 90 percent of wages—to $140,000, phased-in over 10 years—would lower Social Security's projected shortfall by 43 percent.

  This is fair because higher wage earners have recently benefited from substantial tax cuts and other subsidies for their investment and retirement accounts.

- Second, we can diversify Social Security's Trust Fund investments to increase the likelihood of higher returns.

Today, the Trust Fund can only be invested in special Treasury bonds. These are safe investments that currently earn about 6% for the trust funds.

Low-Income Retirees Depend on Social Security

Low-income seniors received 82 percent of their retirement income from Social Security in 2001, while wealthy seniors depended on Social Security for only 19 percent of their income.

Sources of Income for Seniors, 2001

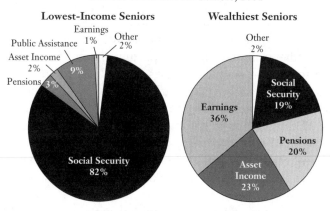

Note: Percentages for low-income seniors do not add to 100 due to rounding.

CQ Researcher, September 24, 2004.

Investing some of Social Security's funds in a broad index fund, like most other pension systems, could yield higher returns. Unlike private accounts, this approach would also spread the risk across the whole population and all generations.

Administrative costs and management fees would be far less than for millions of personal accounts. Diversifying investment in this way could lower the expected shortfall by 15 percent.

Taken together, these two reasonable steps would lower Social Security's shortfall by more than half—and that is just for starters. There are other steps, short of gambling with risky private accounts, that could strengthen the program even more.

Less Security and Less Income

Some proponents present the concept of private accounts in fancy wrapping and colorful ribbons. They are promising a kind of "free lunch"—Social Security changes that come at no cost to anyone.

But, we should remember that all that glitters is not gold. These plans could easily leave you and your children with more debt, less security, and quite probably, less income. That is unacceptable.

There is a lot at stake in this debate. The trillions of dollars it would cost to create a private account system may well lead to higher interest rates that will raise interest payments on all of the federal debt. That would squeeze the federal budget even tighter. It could lead to higher taxes on everyone and cuts in the funding for essential federal programs besides Social Security, such as Medicare and Medicaid.

This would be bad for the economy, bad for family budgets, and bad for future generations.

And it's likely that the next generation would have to pay twice to take this gamble—once to keep our commitments to current retirees, then again to pay into private accounts.

In closing, let me be clear: AARP supports individual accounts. They are an essential savings tool, but in addition to Social Security, not in place of it.

It is extremely important for our children and grandchildren to be setting money aside to invest and save for their retirement. But we need to encourage this saving and investment independent of Social Security.

But, under no circumstances should we weaken Social Security by diverting money from it to create private accounts.

Maintaining America's Principles

This is first and foremost a question of values.

As a nation that values the well-being, dignity and security of every citizen, we should not abandon those principles and leave millions of older Americans at risk.

As a nation that has always recognized that a house divided cannot stand, we should not allow Social Security to become a generational dividing line, pitting old against young.

[Former U.S. president] Franklin Roosevelt said it best during his radio address on Social Security's third anniversary: He said:

" . . . In our efforts to provide security for all American people, let us not allow ourselves to be misled by those who advocate short cuts to Utopia or fantastic financial schemes."

With your help, we will strengthen Social Security and keep its promise now and for generations to come.

Periodical Bibliography

The following articles have been selected to supplement the diverse views presented in this chapter.

Sheryll D. Cashin	"Living Separately and Unequally," *Liberal Opinion Week*, July 19, 2004.
John F. Cogan, R. Glenn Hubbard, and Daniel P. Kessler	"Healthy, Wealthy, and Wise," *Hoover Digest*, Summer 2004.
D'Vera Cohn and Sarah Cohn	"The Doors to Professions Widen," *Washington Post National Weekly Edition*, January 5–11, 2004.
Mary H. Cooper	"Social Security Reform," *CQ Researcher*, September 24, 2004.
Yves Engler	"Rising Health Costs," *Z Magazine*, April 2004.
Claudia Fegan	"Physicians' Rx for an Ailing Healthcare System," *Multinational Monitor*, October 2004.
Samuel Francis	"Sleepers Are Waking Up to Immigration's Impact," *Conservative Chronicle*, February 11, 2004.
Paul T. Hill, Kacey Guin, and Mary Beth Celio	"The Chasm Remains," *Education Next*, Spring 2003.
Kenneth Jost	"School Desegregation," *CQ Researcher*, April 23, 2004.
Colbert I. King	"Slow Progress, 50 Years After Brown," *Liberal Opinion Week*, March 8, 2004.
George W. Lieberman	"Will the U.S. Get Left Behind?" *World & I*, June 2003.
Morton Mintz	"Single-Payer: Good for Business," *Nation*, November 15, 2004.
David J. Weinschrott	"What's Really Wrong with Health Care," *American Outlook*, Spring 2004.
Audrey Williams	"Fundamental Success," *Crisis*, November/December 2003.

CHAPTER 4

What Type of Foreign Policy Should the United States Pursue?

Chapter Preface

In January 2004, U.S. president George W. Bush announced his spending priorities for the fiscal year 2005. According to Bush, nonsecurity-related spending would rise by less than 1 percent in order to help reduce America's growing budget deficit. "By exercising spending discipline in Washington, D.C., we will reduce the deficit and meet our most basic priorities," said Bush. Under his new budget, defense spending would increase by 7 percent. This emphasis on defense spending is the result of national security concerns following the September 11, 2001, terrorist attacks. Indeed, the war on terrorism has become a high priority for the Bush administration. Some analysts contend, however, that the United States is spending huge amounts of money on a war it can never win. With the nation spending more on national security at the expense of domestic programs, commentators wonder whether this shift in policy is wise, and whether it signals a permanent rearrangement in federal spending priorities.

Members of the Bush administration assert that America is winning the war on terrorism. According to Secretary of State Condoleezza Rice, "The United States and our allies are disrupting terrorist operations, cutting off their funding, and hunting down terrorists one-by-one. Their world is getting smaller." Secretary of Defense Donald Rumsfeld states, "It is a war we must win and we will," and George W. Bush asserts, "Make no mistake about it, we are winning, and we will win." They stress that the war will be long and difficult but that victory is possible if the United States commits enough resources to the task. Policy analysts Jack Spencer and Ha Nguyen warn that America must remain committed to this goal. "We'll have to spend billions of dollars and suffer more casualties before we prevail," they say, but "we will continue to thrive even as we hound our enemies until they join the Soviets in the back pages of history books."

Many analysts, however, have a less optimistic outlook on the possibility of winning a war against terrorism. George J. Tenet, former director of the Central Intelligence Agency (CIA), sees no end to the terrorist threats America faces. "The al-Qa'ida [terrorist group] leadership structure . . . is seriously damaged—but the group remains as committed as ever to attacking the U.S. homeland," says Tenet. He adds, "The steady spread of [terrorist leader] Usama bin Ladin's anti-U.S. sentiment . . . ensures that a serious threat will remain for the foreseeable future . . . with or without al-Qa'ida in the picture." Policy analyst Richard C. Leone agrees with Tenet. "The struggle against terrorism could continue for generations," he predicts. According to ex-CIA official Michael Scheuer, this struggle will eventually end in defeat. The war on terror "can't be won," maintains Scheuer. "We're going to eventually lose it." In his opinion, reports that much of al Qaeda's leadership has been destroyed are "ludicrous."

As the United States moves forward in the twenty-first century, there will continue to be debate over what type of foreign policy the country should pursue. The war on terror is only one part of this debate. The following chapter explores the role that democratization should play in America's foreign policy, whether or not the United States should use preemptive force to contain threats, and how the United States should try to mend its relationship with Europe.

"*Democracies do not support terrorists or threaten the world with weapons of mass murder.*"

Spreading Democracy Overseas Will Enhance U.S. Security

George W. Bush

In the following viewpoint George W. Bush asserts that the security of the United States is endangered by the existence of undemocratic nations, particularly those in the Middle East. Until the United States brings democracy to nations such as Jordan and Qatar, it will be threatened by terrorism and weapons of mass murder, he says. According to Bush, the United States is taking many steps to encourage Middle East democracy, such as providing educational materials and business internships to the people there. He believes such actions must be continued and expanded within the framework of a broad policy. Bush is the former governor of Texas and the forty-third president of the United States.

As you read, consider the following questions:

1. According to Bush, what was the "simple truth" that Winston Churchill set before the world?
2. How can the media help advance democracy, as explained by the author?
3. What will the success of democracy in Afghanistan and Iraq show, as argued by Bush?

George W. Bush, speech at Washington, DC, February 4, 2004.

[F]ormer British prime minister Winston] Churchill's 90 years on earth joined together two ages. He stood in the presence of Queen Victoria, who first reigned in 1837. He was the Prime Minister to Elizabeth II, who reigns today [2000]. Sir Winston met [U.S. president] Theodore Roosevelt, and he met [U.S. president] Richard Nixon.

Over his long career, Winston Churchill knew success and he knew failure, but he never passed unnoticed. He was a prisoner in the Boer War, a controversial strategist in the Great War.[1] He was the rallying voice of the Second World War, and a prophet of the Cold War. He helped abolish the sweat shops. He gave coal miners an eight-hour day. He was an early advocate of the tank. And he helped draw boundary lines that remain on the map of the Middle East. He was an extraordinary man.

Helping to Save the World

In spare moments, pacing and dictating to harried secretaries, he produced 15 books. He said, "History will be kind to me—for I intend to write it." History has been kind to Winston Churchill, as it usually is to those who help save the world.

In a decade of political exile during the 1930s, Churchill was dismissed as a nuisance and a crank. When the crisis he predicted arrived, nearly everyone knew that only one man could rescue Britain. The same trait that had made him an outcast eventually made him the leader of his country. Churchill possessed, in one writer's words, an "absolute refusal, unlike many good and prudent men around him, to compromise or to surrender.". . .

When World War II ended, Winston Churchill immediately understood that the victory was incomplete. Half of Europe was occupied by an aggressive empire. And one of Churchill's own finest hours came after the war ended in a speech he delivered in Fulton, Missouri. Churchill warned of the new danger facing free peoples. In stark but measured tones, he spoke of the need for free nations to unite against

1. The Boer wars were fought between the British and the Dutch in South Africa in the late 1800s. World War I is often called the Great War.

communist expansion. [Soviet leader] Marshal [Joseph] Stalin denounced the speech as a "call to war." A prominent American journalist called the speech an "almost catastrophic blunder." In fact, Churchill had set a simple truth before the world: that tyranny could not be ignored or appeased without great risk. And he boldly asserted that freedom—freedom was the right of men and women on both sides of the Iron Curtain.[2]

Churchill understood that the Cold War was not just a standoff of armies, but a conflict of visions—a clear divide between those who put their faith in ideologies of power, and those who put their faith in the choices of free people. The successors of Churchill and [U.S. president Franklin D.] Roosevelt—leaders like [U.S. presidents Harry] Truman, and [Ronald] Reagan, and, [former British prime minister Margaret] Thatcher—led a confident alliance that held firm as communism collapsed under the weight of its own contradictions.

Similar Challenges Today

Today, we are engaged in a different struggle. Instead of an armed empire, we face stateless networks. Instead of massed armies, we face deadly technologies that must be kept out of the hands of terrorists and outlaw regimes.

Yet in some ways, our current struggles or challenges are similar to those Churchill knew. The outcome of the war on terror depends on our ability to see danger and to answer it with strength and purpose. One by one, we are finding and dealing with the terrorists, drawing tight what Winston Churchill called a "closing net of doom." This war also is a conflict of visions. In their worship of power, their deep hatreds, their blindness to innocence, the terrorists are successors to the murderous ideologies of the 20th century. And we are the heirs of the tradition of liberty, defenders of the freedom, the conscience and the dignity of every person. Others before us have shown bravery and moral clarity in

2. The Iron Curtain, a term coined by Churchill in his Fulton speech, was an imaginary boundary that divided Europe into two separate areas of political influence and ideology from the end of World War II to the end of the Cold War.

this cause. The same is now asked of us, and we accept the responsibilities of history.

The tradition of liberty has advocates in every culture and in every religion. Our great challenges support the momentum of freedom in the greater Middle East. The stakes could not be higher. As long as that region is a place of tyranny and despair and anger, it will produce men and movements that threaten the safety of Americans and our friends. We seek the advance of democracy for the most practical of reasons: because democracies do not support terrorists or threaten the world with weapons of mass murder.

America is pursuing a forward strategy of freedom in the Middle East. We're challenging the enemies of reform, confronting the allies of terror, and expecting a higher standard from our friends. For too long, American policy looked away while men and women were oppressed, their rights ignored and their hopes stifled. That era is over, and we can be confident. As in Germany, and Japan, and Eastern Europe, liberty will overcome oppression in the Middle East.

Change from Within

True democratic reform must come from within. And across the Middle East, reformers are pushing for change. From Morocco, to Jordan, to Qatar, we're seeing elections and new protections for women and the stirring of political pluralism. When the leaders of reform ask for our help, America will give it.

I've asked the Congress to double the budget for the National Endowment for Democracy, raising its annual total to $80 million. We will focus its new work on bringing free elections and free markets and free press and free speech and free labor unions to the Middle East. The National Endowment gave vital service in the Cold War, and now we are renewing its mission of freedom in the war on terror.

Freedom of the press and the free flow of ideas are vital foundations of liberty. To cut through the hateful propaganda that fills the airwaves in the Muslim world and to promote open debate, we're broadcasting the message of tolerance and truth in Arabic and Persian to tens of millions. In some cities of the greater Middle East, our radio stations are rated number one amongst younger listeners. Next week [February 2004] we will launch a new Middle East television network called, Alhurra—Arabic for "the free one." The network will broadcast news and movies and sports and entertainment and educational programming to millions of people across the region. Through all these efforts, we are telling the people in the Middle East the truth about the values and the policies of the United States, and the truth always serves the cause of freedom.

A Ticking Time Bomb

The problem is stark. The Arab world is the only major region that does not have a single democracy. If we look at the Middle East in general, only Israel and Turkey are democracies. Of the 16 Arab states, only Lebanon has ever been a democracy, and only a few could be described today as even semi-democratic. Whereas the rest of the world has been moving toward democracy and greater freedom over the past three remarkable decades, the Arab world has remained politically stagnant. In fact, the Arab region is the only part of the world where the average . . . rating of political rights and civil liberties is worse today than it was in 1974. . . .

A growing number of Arab scholars, journalists, civic activists, and even some government officials, as well as numerous foreign observers of the region, are becoming convinced that the center cannot hold without democratizing.

Larry Diamond, *Hoover Digest*, Winter 2005.

America is also taking the side of reformers who have begun to change the Middle East. We're providing loans and business advice to encourage a culture of entrepreneurship in the Middle East. We've established business internships for women, to teach them the skills of enterprise, and to help them achieve social and economic equality. We're supporting the work of judicial reformers who demand independent courts and the rule of law. At the request of countries in the region, we're providing Arabic language textbooks to boys and girls. We're helping education reformers improve their school systems.

The message to those who long for liberty and those who work for reform is that they can be certain they have a strong ally, a constant ally in the United States of America.

Our strategy and our resolve are being tested in two countries, in particular. The nation of Afghanistan was once the primary training ground of [the terrorist group] al Qaeda, the home of a barbaric regime called the Taliban. It now has a new constitution that guarantees free election and full participation by women.

The nation of Iraq was for decades an ally of terror ruled by the cruelty and caprice of one man. Today, the people of Iraq are moving toward self-government.[3] Our coalition is working with the Iraqi Governing Council to draft a basic law with a bill of rights. Because our coalition acted, terrorists lost a source of reward money for suicide bombings. Because we acted, nations of the Middle East no longer need to fear reckless aggression from a ruthless dictator who had the intent and capability to inflict great harm on his people and people around the world. [Former Iraqi president] Saddam Hussein now sits in a prison cell, and Iraqi men and women are no longer carried to torture chambers and rape rooms, and dumped in mass graves. Because the Baathist regime is history, Iraq is no longer a grave and gathering threat to free nations. Iraq is a free nation.

Enemies of Freedom

Freedom still has enemies in Afghanistan and Iraq. All the Baathists and Taliban and terrorists know that if democracy were to be, it would undermine violence—their hope for violence and innocent death. They understand that if democracy were to be undermined, then the hopes for change throughout the Middle East would be set back. That's what they know. That's what they think. We know that the success of freedom in these nations would be a landmark event in the history of the Middle East, and the history of the world. Across the region, people would see that freedom is the path to progress and national dignity. A thousand lies would stand refuted, falsehoods about the incompatibility of democratic values in Middle Eastern cultures. And all would see, in Afghanistan and Iraq, the success of free institutions at the heart of the greater Middle East.

3. Iraq held free elections in 2005.

Achieving this vision will be the work of many nations over time, requiring the same strength of will and confidence of purpose that propelled freedom to victory in the defining struggles of the last century. Today, we're at a point of testing, when people and nations show what they're made out of. America will never be intimidated by thugs and assassins. We will do what it takes. We will not leave until the job is done.

We will succeed because when given a choice, people everywhere, from all walks of life, from all religions, prefer freedom to violence and terror. We will succeed because human beings are not made by the Almighty God to live in tyranny. We will succeed because of who we are—because even when it is hard, Americans always do what is right.

And we know the work that has fallen to this generation. When great striving is required of us, we will always have an example in the man we honor today. Winston Churchill was a man of extraordinary personal gifts, yet his greatest strength was his unshakable confidence in the power and appeal of freedom. It was the great fortune of mankind that he was there in an hour of peril. And it remains the great duty of mankind to advance the cause of freedom in our time.

"Democracy is not a necessary condition for U.S. security."

Spreading Democracy Overseas Will Not Enhance U.S. Security

Gerard Alexander

In the following viewpoint Gerard Alexander warns that a general policy of spreading democracy throughout the world is not the best way to ensure America's security. While it may be beneficial to bring democracy to some nations, says Alexander, there is no proof that all authoritarian countries are a threat to the United States. In fact, he argues, failing to address the real causes of anti-Western extremism may lead to an increase in regimes hostile to the United States. He advises that America be cautious and selective in its attempts to spread democracy. Alexander is associate professor of politics at the University of Virginia and author of *The Sources of Democratic Consolidation*.

As you read, consider the following questions:
1. What is the "authoritarian radicalization thesis," as explained by the author?
2. As exemplified by Great Britain, what can happen to authoritarian regimes over time, in Alexander's opinion?
3. According to the author, what often happens when a dictatorship falls?

The belief that non-democratic regimes incubate anti-Western extremism, making their aggrieved populations vulnerable to recruitment by terrorist groups, is the principal assumption behind the democracy project, which argues that it is in America's compelling interest to promote democratic regimes wherever possible. Given its impact on policy, this assumption deserves scrutiny. While it is true that several authoritarian societies have bred anti-Western extremism, many others have not. Sympathy for democracy does not constitute sufficient grounds for a sweeping policy of worldwide democratization.

The United States does not require a fully democratic world in order to achieve security. Indeed, the threats we currently face are generated by causes that transcend regime type. Moreover, an ambitious policy of democratization may have high opportunity costs, because the vast resources that would have to be allocated could not be used for attacking the factors which are generating anti-Western extremism.

Favoring democratization is, of course, not a new feature of U.S. international policy. The United States has a lengthy history of close alliances with and support for democracies. But it is well known that the United States also formed durable, peaceful relationships and even partnerships with many authoritarian regimes. This mixture of regime types among America's allies was true both in desperate times and distant regions and in more ordinary times and regions of core interest, including within NATO [North Atlantic Treaty Organization].

It was also matched by a mix of regime types on the roster of America's perceived adversaries. This is not surprising given that throughout the 20th century, American foreign policy leaders traced major security threats to factors that cut across regime type. Some non-democratic regimes were expansionist, including Nazi Germany, the USSR [Union of Soviet Socialist Republics], North Korea and Saddam [Hussein]'s Iraq. But many more were not. It is no coincidence that even the [Ronald] Reagan Administration—seen today by democratizers as an exemplary precursor to their current effort—continued to work closely with many authoritarian regimes against the USSR. Rhetorically, the administration advanced [foreign policy adviser] Jeane Kirkpatrick's well-known distinction between widely varying non-democratic regimes. Kirkpatrick explicitly argued that this variation permitted the United States to prioritize since it could afford to view quite a few of these regimes relatively benignly and only some of them with urgent concern. . . .

Authoritarian Radicalization

While the 1990s saw an increase in support for democracies around the world, it was after the September 11 [2001] terrorist attacks that the democratizing agenda received a massive boost. Senior [George W.] Bush Administration officials and neoconservative theorists have argued that non-democratic regimes serve as incubators of grievances, which then can be politicized by anti-Western extremists. [Columnist] Charles Krauthammer, even while recommending selective democratization for now, says that ultimately "the spread of democracy is . . . an indispensable means for securing American interests." President [George W.] Bush declared in a November 2002 speech to the National Endowment for Democracy (NED) that accommodating non-democratic regimes in the Middle East may have created allies in the short term but "did nothing to make us safe" over the longer run, because these regimes were breeding "stagnation, resentment and violence ready for export." Bush's 2004 State of the Union speech was even more specific: "As long as the Middle East remains a place of tyranny and despair and anger, it will continue to produce men and movements that threaten the safety of America and our friends." This might be called the "authoritarian radicalization" thesis. . . .

The thesis proposes that authoritarianism is inherently radicalizing and that democracy is inherently moderating, thus generating a policy prescription for global democratization. The 2002 National Security Strategy makes it a national priority to promote "modern government, especially in the Muslim world", in order to undermine the "fertile ground" that exists for "the conditions and ideologies that promote terrorism." [In late 2004] Bush has proposed a further doubling of the NED budget, telling the NED that the United States has adopted "a forward strategy of freedom in the Middle East." And he has declared his hope that Iraq will democratize the region through a contagion effect.

Reasons Not to Democratize

But there are compelling reasons not to translate this thesis into a sweeping agenda. These reasons concern the high degree of diversity that exists among non-democratic regimes; the risks that can accompany pushing dictators from office; and the potential opportunity costs of a democratization policy.

Diversity within the category of "authoritarian" is enormous, with implications for U.S. foreign policy. The intention here is not to find virtue in authoritarianism, only to emphasize that while some non-democratic regimes appear to be incubators of radicalization, most do not, just as most have not warred with America. No clear pattern connects non-democratic regimes to extremist, violent or anti-Western ideologies.

In the 1970s, radical ideologies and movements flourished in non-democratic Nicaragua, El Salvador, Guatemala and Iran. Since the 1980s, this degenerative dynamic was apparent in Algeria, Egypt, Saudi Arabia, Afghanistan, military-ruled Pakistan and the Israeli-occupied Palestinian territories. Some of these regimes tolerated or even subsidized propagandizing and proselytizing with an extremist content that was often disseminated through institutions and activities usually described optimistically as "civil society."

Yet this roster of regimes does not come close to exhausting the list of all non-democratic regimes even in the Muslim world. And while proponents of the authoritarian radicalization thesis point to trends in Saudi Arabia or Pakistan to make their case, they are unable to explain why other indisputably authoritarian regimes in the region such as Morocco, Tunisia, Kuwait and Jordan have been able to contain [terrorist group] Al-Qaeda-style movements. Furthermore, nearly two dozen predominantly or substantially Muslim societies in Saharan and sub-Saharan Africa or in southwestern and Central Asia have been authoritarian for decades, yet extremism is notable for its weakness there. Studies warn that radicalization could happen in these regions, but it has not.

References to the "poisonous cultural effects of tyranny" notwithstanding, authoritarianism seems to generate political extremism in some Muslim settings but not in others.

Dangerous Strategy

[George W.] Bush is plainly urging democracy not only on hostile powers such as Syria and Iran but also on traditional "friends" such as Egypt and Saudi Arabia. . . .

To describe this as ambitious is to be guilty of understatement. If such a grand strategy were to be pursued without extreme care and subtlety, it would risk producing regimes hostile to the U.S. and hospitable to terrorism—in between periods of anarchy—in a vital strategic and economic region. Admittedly, such regimes already exist, and periods of anarchy occur there from time to time. But prudence should warn us against adding to the problem. Nor is it sensible to inform such regimes they have nothing to lose by opposing us since we are determined to overthrow them in any event.

John O'Sullivan, *National Review*, December 22, 2003.

A mixed pattern also characterizes Latin America, where several military regimes may have inspired leftist insurgencies in the 1960s and 1970s but other regimes did not. Perhaps most unexpectedly, totalitarian regimes do not seem to generate popular radicalism over the long term. Marxist-Leninist states and, ironically, Ba'athi rule in Iraq,[1] may leave citizens ideologically exhausted and cynical rather than motivated and ripe for recruitment. Overall, the authoritarian radicalization thesis seems especially weak in post-colonial sub-Saharan Africa, one of the most pervasively non-democratic regions, but also one in which extremisms of any kind have found few followers.

Another universe of cases must be considered as well. The authoritarian radicalization thesis, to be taken seriously, also has to be tested against the non-democratic regimes that dominated Europe for centuries. Some of these regimes could be said to have incubated communism, socialism or fascism. But mass politics under other European authoritarian regimes moderated with time rather than becoming rad-

1. The Ba'ath political party ruled Iraq from 1963 to 2003.

icalized, with Britain as the paradigmatic example. Most of the world's most stable democracies—the very societies which are now said to be threatened by the existence of authoritarian regimes elsewhere—themselves evolved from historic non-democratic regimes which gave way to societies among the most politically moderate the world has ever known. In other words, authoritarian regimes are capable, over time, of creating liberal institutions that can lay the groundwork for a transition to democracy without significant external intervention.

This also shows that authoritarianism is not a sufficient condition for extremism. It may also not be a necessary one. Al-Qaeda-type beliefs have found support among at least some Muslims in democratic Turkey and western Europe. By that same standard, militant Islamist networks appear to have steadily grown in Pakistan in the 1980s and 1990s under both authoritarian and democratic rule alike. For that matter, Northern Ireland has had democratic rights but for decades has also harbored a subculture of resentment, violence and radicalism that generated a steady stream of terrorists.

None of this is to find virtue in authoritarianism. Non-democratic regimes are often ugly and corrupt, and people are usually better off living under democracy. But authoritarianism as a general category does not breed extremism. It is not even obvious that any specific authoritarian sub-type does that. This has a central implication: Democracy is not a necessary condition for U.S. security.

Opportunity Costs

Why not pursue democratization anyway? There are two important reasons for the United States to pursue a highly selective democratization policy rather than an urgent and universalistic one. Jeane Kirkpatrick long ago offered the first of these. Her 1979 essay emphasized not only that non-democracies are highly varied, but also that America was—and remains today—unsure how to fine-tune either regime changes or regime-stabilization. In combination, these points mean that when a dictatorship falls (including when pushed), it can be followed by a regime that is better, the same, or much worse, and we often cannot do much to influence which it will be. In Iraq in 1958, Cuba in 1959, Iran during 1978–79, and Nicaragua during 1979–80, non-democratic regimes were replaced by even worse ones. This is not a reason to abandon democratization. But it is a reason to pursue democratization carefully and selectively.

Finally, high opportunity costs should give us pause. If democracy really could undercut popular support for anti-Western extremism, the United States might well be justified in mounting a resource-, time- and attention-consuming project of worldwide democratization. But as we have seen, Al-Qaeda-style extremism has drawn strong support in some authoritarian-ruled Muslim countries but not in many others. This suggests that something (or things) other than regime type is crucial to fuelling violent anti-Western extremism. In that case, a costly democratization project could easily leave that "something" unaddressed. At the very least, acknowledging that the causes of violent extremism transcend regime type would free us up to ask what they might be.

Soviet-dissident-turned-Israeli-politician Natan Sharansky offers a parallel. He had long believed that antisemitism in the USSR was caused by totalitarianism. If Russia democratized, he expected it to disappear. But the resilience of antisemitism in post-Soviet Russia—not to mention in western Europe—has forced Sharansky to conclude that the causes of antisemitism lay elsewhere, in places left undiscovered while he was mistakenly focused on regime type.

Selective Democratization

This analysis has three implications. First, it suggests that democratization should not be raised to the level of urgent, universal principle and should instead be pursued selectively (as, it must be acknowledged, the Bush Administration has done so far). In 1979, Kirpatrick argued that pressures to democratize were characterized by too much of a double standard, since more was being done to undermine authoritarian regimes friendly to the United States than more brutal and hostile totalitarian regimes. The risk today is rather of a single standard, treating all non-democratic regimes as sources of security threats, when in fact non-democratic regimes are as varied as ever. What is needed now is a sharp distinction between non-democratic regimes that are incubators of radicalism and ones that are not.

Second, it means that alongside highly selective democratization, we need to investigate what causes we really do think are generating extremist ideologies. It is critical to remember that Islamic extremism, for example, has found fertile soil within most of Europe's advanced industrial democracies. This debate is today only in its infancy, but it is no less urgent than fighting already crystallized terrorist groups. Rather than focusing solely on regime type, it might concern Wahhabi proselytizing; or dangerously reduced levels of American public diplomacy; or the peculiar dynamics of authoritarianism or democratization in certain countries that either advances or retards radicalization. We will not come to firmer conclusions until we make this a central focus of our thinking.

Ironically, all this is actually good news for U.S. policy in Iraq. Even if U.S. intervention does not create a stable democracy there, U.S. security may well be substantially enhanced even if Iraq develops a relatively benign though authoritarian regime. Such a regime could easily maintain durably peaceful relations with the United States, would not support terrorism, and might well not incubate extremism. And Iraq was an inspired candidate for selective democratization, since it would be very difficult to result in a worse regime. Saddam was not a run-of-the-mill dictator but one of the pre-eminent genocidal rulers of the second half of the 20th century, who posed a real threat to the well-being of his neighbors and the entire international system. In at least some cases, giving a tyrant a push is undeniably a good thing.

*"A failure to preempt is often far worse
than the act itself."*

U.S. Foreign Policy Should Be Based on Preemption and Unilateralism

Victor Davis Hanson

While America's use of preemption and unilateralism following the terrorist attacks of September 11, 2001, have been widely criticized, these policies are effective in protecting America from future attacks, maintains Victor Davis Hanson in the following viewpoint. He argues that history shows the wisdom of striking first before threats became unmanageable, and he contends that it would be dangerous for America not to use its power to protect itself. Hanson has written essays, editorials, and reviews for numerous publications, including the *New York Times*, the *Wall Street Journal*, the *International Herald Tribune*, and the *New York Post*. He is a weekly columnist for the *National Review Online*.

As you read, consider the following questions:
1. How is preemption much like confronting the school bully, as explained by Hanson?
2. In the author's opinion, how is the strength of the U.S. military related to criticisms of unilateralism?
3. Why are United Nations' sanctions ineffective, as argued by Hanson?

"**P**reemption" is supposed to be the new slur. Its use now conjures up all sorts of Dr. Strangelove[1] images to denigrate the present "trigger-happy" Bush administration. Partly the hysteria is due to the invasion of Iraq [in 2003]. Or perhaps the venom of the Left comes from recent disclosures that, in the [era after the September 11, 2001, terrorist attacks], the United States has publicly proclaimed it may strike terrorists and their sponsors—or indeed rogue nations who have the history, capability, and desire to obtain frightening weapons—before they strike us.

But instead of a rational discussion about the wisdom and feasibility of that logical policy, we have had two years now [as of January 2004] of national frenzy over a purported new "dangerous departure" in American foreign policy, one that "threatens" to "destabilize" the world order.

A Centuries-Old Concept

Rubbish. Preemption is a concept as old as the Greeks. It perhaps was first articulated in the fourth book of [ancient Greek historian] Thucydides's history. There the veteran Theban general Pagondas explained why his Boeotians should hit the Athenians at the border near Delium, even though they were already retreating and posed no immediate threat. The Boeotians did, and won—and were never attacked by the Athenians again. On a more immediate level, preemption was how many of us stayed alive in a rather tough grade school: Confront the bully first, openly, and in daylight—our Texan principal warned us—before he could jump you as planned in the dark on the way home.

Despite the current vogue of questionable and therapeutic ideas like "zero tolerance" and "moral equivalence" that punish all who use force—whether in kindergarten or in the Middle East—striking first is a morally neutral concept. It takes on its ethical character from the landscape in which it takes place—the Israelis bombing the Iraqi reactor to avoid being blackmailed by a soon-to-be nuclear Saddam Hussein, or the French going into the Ivory Coast last year [2003] de-

---

1. In this 1964 film an insane American general orders a nuclear attack on the Soviet Union.

spite the fact that that chaotic country posed no immediate danger to Paris.[2] The thing to keep in mind is that the real aggressor, by his past acts, has already invited war and will do so again—should he be allowed to choose his own time and place of assault.

Necessary Actions

[Adolf] Hitler was ruthless in starting a war against Poland. Yet he could have been stopped far earlier in 1936 or so—had the democracies preempted him. Indeed, a failure to preempt is often far worse than the act itself. Serbia posed no "imminent" threat to the United States in 1998; but President [Bill] Clinton—with no U.N. [United Nations] sanction, no U.S. Congress resolution—finally decided to act and end that cancer [of genocide in Bosnia] before it spread beyond the Balkans.

Nor has the United States established "a dangerous precedent" in hitting Saddam Hussein before he could add any more corpses to his three-decade-long record of carnage. Turkey did not jump back into Cyprus. We did not move on to hit Havana. Pakistan and India are now talking—not in smoke amid cinders. Neither was emboldened by the three-week war—as shrill critics in the United States promised—to strike the other first.[3] No front-line Arab state saw the March 2003 attacks as an invitation to bomb Israel, now convinced that the United States has sanctified first-strike strategy.

Nor is preemption always even a sign of strength. Italy regretted its 1940 surprise invasion of Greece [where it was defeated and pushed back into Albania], Argentina tried it in the Falklands [in 1982] and paid a high price [with many lives lost and prisoners taken]; so did Syria in 1973 [when it unsuccessfully attempted to take control of the Golan Heights], and al Qaeda and the Taliban on September 11 [2001].[4] Up until now, when democratic states took preemp-

2. In 1981 Israel bombed and destroyed the Osiraq nuclear reactor near Baghdad in an attempt to prevent Iraq from developing nuclear weapons. In response to military and civil unrest in 2003, France sent troops to the Ivory Coast to help maintain ceasefire boundaries.   3. In 2003 a U.S.-led coalition invaded Iraq and deposed Iraqi leader Saddam Hussein, creating fears that other countries would follow its example of preemptive war.   4. Following terrorist group al Qaeda's September 11 attack, America launched a war on terrorism, which continues as of this writing.

tory action against fascists and succeeded, the doctrine was largely ignored in silent satisfaction. Yet when autocracies have invaded other democratic states, or democratic states have failed in their anticipatory efforts, then it was roundly condemned as a flawed concept. The wisdom of preemption was determined relatively; having a good cause and achieving success, it seems, made it worthwhile. What is new is the absolutist, blanket condemnation of the strategy altogether.

Eternal Vigilance

The lesson of history is that to secure our liberty, America must be constantly on guard, preparing to defend our nation against tomorrow's adversaries even as we vanquish the enemies of today.

Over the past decade, America let down her guard. With the collapse of the Soviet Union, our leaders assumed that the post-Cold War world would be one of unlimited peace and prosperity, and that our greatest security challenges would be invading Haiti, or stopping wars in places like Bosnia and Kosovo. The Clinton people slashed our defense budget in search of a "peace dividend," while sending our forces all over the world on a plethora of missions that drained America's military readiness. They put off investments needed to prepare for the real emerging threats to U.S. national security. Instead of focusing on new dangers, they spent their time and energy forging ridiculous new treaties. . . .

In the wake of [the September 11, 2001, terrorist attacks] a measure of sanity has been restored to debates over U.S. foreign policy. Awakened to new dangers, our challenge is now twofold: First, we must win the war on terrorism that took our nation by surprise. And second, we must prepare now for the threats that could emerge to surprise us in the decades ahead.

Jesse Helms, *Imprimis*, January 2002.

In short, preemption is now a politicized, debased word. It is part of the anti-Bush lexicon and has lost any real meaning for the foreseeable future of its usage. The same may be true of "multilateralism" and "unilateralism."

A Meaningless Word

Perhaps the greatest example of "multilateral" military action was the Nazi invasion of the Soviet Union. Think of the vast multilateral coalition! Germans, Austrians, Romanians, Czechs, Finns, Spaniards, Bulgarians, and Italians all united together to attack Communist Russia, which in turn had no other combatants on its front but unilaterally-minded Russians.

In 1939 Great Britain was a unilateral power, threatened by a broad multilateral axis and without any real ally. The 1956 Suez Crisis was a multilateral enterprise—an undertaking by France, Great Britain, and Israel. It was stopped unilaterally by the Eisenhower administration.[5] Israel in 1973 reacted unilaterally to a preemptive strike from a multilateral coalition involving Egypt, Jordan, Syria, Lebanon, and Iraq. The only real constant was not preemption/multilateralism/unilateralism, but simply that a democratic state was fighting those who were not.

Allies themselves are not always wonderful assets: Dozens of coalition members helped Hitler butcher thousands of Ukrainians and enabled the Soviets to spread worldwide terror [during World War II]. Too many allies were largely the reason that we did not go to Baghdad in 1991 and take out Saddam Hussein when it would have been far easier—and would have spared the lives of thousands long since dead.[6] The European Union had gads of countries in a truly multilateral coalition, only to watch a quarter-million Bosnians and Kosovars die [in genocide there during the 1990s] until a unilateral United States intervened.

Of course, today multilateralism is deemed "good," while unilateralism is "bad" because, in the unipolar, post–Cold War era, the United States has a military monopoly unparalleled in civilization's history. For good or evil it alone can alter political situations rather rapidly through use of its military power, while friends and enemies alike flock publicly to the U.N. to object—or flock privately to us to ask for help.

The Left's problem is not our embrace of the concept of "unilateralism" per se—or it would have attacked [former

5. This 1956 war broke out between Egypt—the site of the Suez Canal—and France, Great Britain, and Israel, who wanted economic and trading interests in the canal. The United States forced France and Great Britain to withdraw.   6. In 1990 Iraq invaded Kuwait. A U.S.-led coalition drove Iraqi forces out of that country, but did not try to overthrow Iraqi president Saddam Hussein.

president] Clinton's U.N.-be-damned use of force in Iraq, Kosovo, and Haiti. No, the rub is something altogether different. A Christian, southern-accented, conservative Republican president, coming off a disputed election, has chosen to preempt. And when you hit first in a therapeutic America, you are at least supposed to bite your lip and squeeze [U.S. senator Hillary Clinton's] hand on national television [as President Clinton did]. You do not dare say, "Bring 'em on" and "Smoke 'em out"—much less fly a jet out to an aircraft carrier [as President Bush did]. . . .

Unfounded Criticism

So like preemption, in today's super-charged political climate, unilateralism and multilateralism no longer convey any meaning. Those words too have now become little more than coded nomenclature to denigrate the present American administration's efforts in Afghanistan and Iraq. . . .

President Bush . . . is not getting praise for his courageous attempt at ending the political and cultural climate that led to September 11. The present bastardization of our language proves it.

*"Foreign policy . . . [should] be based on a
commitment to multilateralism and the
rule of international law, on peacemaking
not warmaking."*

U.S. Foreign Policy Should Not Be Based on Preemption and Unilateralism

Craig Eisendrath

In the following viewpoint Craig Eisendrath warns that
America's use of preemption and unilateralism are under-
mining a system of international cooperation that has previously been effective at preventing global violence. Rather
than participating in effective international organizations
and becoming a signatory to global agreements, the United
States is using its superior military power to pursue its own
interests, claims Eisendrath. He claims that America is making the world far more dangerous for everyone by acting
alone and pursuing a policy of preemptive strikes against nations that pose a threat. Eisendrath is a senior fellow at the
Center for International Policy in Washington, D.C.

As you read, consider the following questions:
1. According to Eisendrath, in the period following World
   War II, what premise had been accepted by the United
   States and much of the global community?
2. What was the result of a lack of U.S. support for the
   United Nations in the 1990s, as argued by the author?
3. How has the United States seriously weakened arms
   control, according to Eisendrath?

In 2001, the United States went to war against Afghanistan, arguing that a military strike against the Taliban government was fundamental self-defense after the traumatic terrorist attacks in New York City, Washington, D.C., and Pennsylvania [on September 11]. Although it might have pursued a diplomatic option, such as recourse to the International Court of Justice, the United States received international support and even greater international sympathy. Masses and marches all over the world expressed profound sadness for what had taken place. The French newspaper *Le Monde* demonstrated unprecedented empathy with the banner headline, "We Are All Americans."

In 2003, the United States again went to war; on this occasion, however, there was virtually no international sympathy for the United States, and little international support for its actions. The political positions of both British prime minister Tony Blair and U.S. president George W. Bush further suffered when it was demonstrated that both Washington and London had lied at the highest levels to gain congressional and parliamentary support for the decision to go to war, both on the issue of weapons of mass destruction and on the supposed ties between the 9-11 terrorists and [former Iraqi president] Saddam Hussein.

It became apparent in the immediate post-invasion period that the U.S. decision to wage full-scale war against Iraq had been both rash and senseless. It ignored the fundamental premise of geopolitics that force should be a last resort, after all other options have been tried. Iraq posed no near-term threat to the United States or to U.S. interests. Yet the Bush administration made no attempt to use diplomacy or to build a coalition. Rather, it approached the issue of Iraq assuming that, as the world's dominant military power, it had no need to gain the cooperation of the world community that was organized to meet such international challenges.

A Violent, Self-Serving Policy

While the United States has used its military power in various ways for decades, the Bush administration's unapologetic use of first-strike war as policy is unprecedented. The ostensible rationale has been the post-September-11 "war on terrorism," but in fact, what has come to be known as the "Bush doctrine" reflects a foreign policy approach championed for a decade by neoconservatives. . . .

Reflecting the neoconservative vision, the Bush doctrine proclaims that what the United States, as the world's only surviving superpower, does in pursuit of its own interests is not only right, but good for the rest of the world. Even more insidiously, this vision is based on close working relationships between large corporations and the government, with little thought for the rest of the population of this country or the world. What is good for Halliburton (Vice President [Richard] Cheney's former company and recipient of massive post-war contracts in Iraq) translates directly into benefits for those in power. The installation of several neoconservatives at the beginning of the Bush presidency meant that this violent, self-serving policy would be carried out. World events such as 9-11 are simply the excuse for implementing these pre-determined policies.

Not only has history shown that preemptive use of force eventually does not work, but it flouts the most basic understanding of Judeo-Christian ethics, which require us to listen to others, talk, and seek reconciliation first. Even the most rudimentary just-war theology sees force as a last resort, and only for self-defense.

Former Success of Multilateralism

To fully grasp the current crisis of global violence, we need to understand how dramatically U.S. foreign policy shifted with the 2000 elections and the rise to power of the Bush administration.

In the period following the Second World War, much of the global community, including the United States, had accepted the premise that diplomacy was not just another option, but the primary means by which nations worked to create collective security. Military force was used only when diplomacy failed. The United States helped in pioneering a system of worldwide diplomacy—of which the United Nations was a central element—which worked to foster increasing cooperation among nations along a broad front of peace-keeping as well as political, social, and economic programs. . . .

This fundamental principle of multilateralism and, in particular, the United Nations, have been key targets of the Bush administration. Conservatives have long disdained multilateralism. Following the 1994 Congressional election, a triumph for conservative Republicans, the guiding philosophy of U.S. foreign policy began to shift toward unilateralism. The first victim of this policy was our relationship with the United Nations. In the 1990s, Congressional conservatives, led by Senator Jesse Helms, withheld U.N. dues and peacekeeping assessments and adamantly refused to even consider the establishment of a readily deployable U.N. force for peacekeeping operations. Without such a force, the United Nations remained unable to meet many of the challenges to which it should have been able to respond—including crises in the Balkans, Africa, and the Middle East. The failure of President Bill Clinton to support sending French troops to Rwanda in 1994 contributed to one of the worst holocausts in history.[1]

The Bush administration has continued and exacerbated this erosion of U.S. support for the United Nations. In Iraq, particularly, the United States chose to go ahead with an invasion without the United Nations or a supporting Security Council resolution, to cut off U.N. inspections, and to give the world organization only a nominal role in the provision of aid, economic and social reconstruction, and the formation of a new Iraqi government—accepting U.N. support only at the last minute and then quite grudgingly.

Economic Aid as Foreign Policy

Another important feature of post–World War II U.S. foreign policy was the use of economic aid. The billions of dollars expended through the Marshall Plan fostered a peaceful, viable Western Europe, which was helpful not only in our struggle against communism, but also in providing a rich, democratic life for its citizens.[2] Here, too, the Bush admin-

1. In 1994 Rwandan president Juvénal Habyarimana was assassinated and over the next three months the military and militia killed over one million Rwandans, forcing millions more to flee the country.   2. Following World War II, the United States contributed more than $13 billion of economic and technical assistance to a number of European countries that had been devastated by the war.

istration has enacted a dramatic reversal.

Despite the chronic need for economic aid in Afghanistan, the United States has continuously refused to give this impoverished nation the support it needs to effect economic recovery. As a result, Afghanistan continues to suffer widespread hunger, disease, and economic despair. In 2002, Afghanistan again became the world's leading supplier of heroin. The U.S.-imposed government has not established jurisdiction beyond the suburbs of Kabul (except in a few scattered areas), and [former Afghanistan ruling power] Taliban and [terrorist group] al Qaeda forces have returned to southeastern Afghanistan. Everywhere else in the country, warlords reign.

Bush Diplomacy

BALDINGER 2/26 2005
People's Weekly World

Baldinger. © 2005 by David Baldinger. Reproduced by permission.

In Iraq, a similar pattern of economic neglect in favor of military dominance has meant that Iraqis are seeing little or no economic progress post-invasion. The cost of maintaining the U.S. military force in 2003 was more than fifty times what was spent on non-military support. Here, the lesson of the Marshall Plan at the end of World War II is being lost: Economic reconstruction must follow military victory if peace and stability are to be restored. The nominal transfer of power to a provisional Iraqi government will have little or no effect on these economic realities.

Even beyond Afghanistan and Iraq, the United States' record on international aid is deplorable. It extends only one-tenth of one percent of its GNP [gross national product] to international assistance—far below other developed countries. Thus, the richest country in the world ranks among the stingiest in helping the planet's poor. Conditions that breed war are being neglected throughout the developing world. This represents not only bad policy but bad ethics. "What you do for the least of them, you do for me." (Matt. 25–45).

While insisting on free trade, the United States has maintained high tariffs and subsidies for its agricultural products, making it difficult for developing countries to feed their populations. Through its strong influence on international lending institutions, such as the International Monetary Fund and World Bank, the United States has imposed policies that have decreased living standards in the developing world in favor of protecting the financial community.

Ignoring International Law

A third major shift in the Bush administration is its backing away from the U.S. commitment to international law. Rather than dealing with suspected terrorists captured during the Afghanistan war through the mechanism of international law, the U.S. government opted for its own military tribunals and the suspension of accepted judicial procedures. In doing so, it rejected established judicial structures, such as the United Nations' International Court of Justice, which could have provided a legal procedure based on international law. It rejected established judicial civil procedures that guarantee the rights of the accused, including the right to know the charges, to be represented by an attorney, to have a speedy trial, and to have access to evidence and witnesses for defense. At Guantanamo [naval base in Cuba] and other bases in the United States and abroad, and particularly in Iraq, it has permitted or sanctioned torture in defiance of the Geneva Conventions.[3] Whether recent Supreme Court decisions will curb these violations remains to be seen.

3. In 2004 there were reports of abuse and torture of prisoners at Abu Ghraib prison in Iraq by U.S. armed forces. There have also been allegations of torture and abuse at the U.S. Guantanamo Bay prison in Cuba.

In another dramatic repudiation of international law, the United States—the country that helped conduct the Nuremberg trials [of Nazi war criminals], pioneered the U.N.'s Universal Declaration of Human Rights, and advanced the idea that the world community could define crimes against humanity—refused to join the International Criminal Court (ICC). This tribunal, created in 2003, was supported by every major country in the world. The U.S. objection was that American citizens might be tried for international crimes, even though the ICC Charter clearly stipulates that the court will not try individuals whose countries will do this job themselves. Not only has the United States refused to participate in the ICC, it has done virtually everything it can to undermine the Court's authority by negotiating agreements with individual states in order to prevent the extradition of U.S. citizens to be tried by the Court. It has refused to grant desperately needed economic aid to countries in Asia and Africa unless they agree to these conditions.

The United States has also pulled away from signing international conventions on the rights of children and women and on climate control. As a substitute for international law, the Bush administration proclaimed the United States will consider the preemptive use of nuclear weapons against non-nuclear states and that it will consider military action against any state that might challenge us. In so doing, it has repudiated the standard of the U.N. Charter (particularly Article 51) that force can only be used in self-defense. In general, the United States has rejected or withdrawn from international agreements that restrict U.S. military modernization, including the Comprehensive Nuclear Test Ban, the 1972 Anti-Ballistic Missile Treaty, and pacts on biological weapons, small arms, and land mines. In this way, it has seriously weakened international arms control. Also, in opposition to U.N. resolutions, the Bush administration is planning to develop outer space as a new theater of direct military activity by deploying a missile-defense system, the first installment of which will begin this fall [2004]. It is seeking to create small nuclear devices that will inevitably require a resumption of underground nuclear testing.

Spurred on by these developments, a number of states appear to be moving more aggressively toward their own nuclear capacity, particularly North Korea, and possibly Iran. Tearing up the fabric of arms control created over a fifty-year period puts our security and that of the world in jeopardy.

A further sign of the neoconservative vision of policy based on force rather than diplomacy or international law is the Bush administration's dramatic increase in military spending. The U.S. military budget has ballooned to almost $500 billion (if special expenditures are considered), reversing a trend prior to the fall of the Soviet Union.

It's not just the dollars. Led by Secretary of Defense Donald Rumsfeld, the Department of Defense has moved aggressively to eclipse the State Department as the major locus of our foreign policy. The diplomacy of the State Department has increasingly been ignored; funding for the State Department has become so meager that it has had to close consulates around the world and assign personnel of the well-funded CIA [Central Intelligence Agency] to its diplomatic and consular posts, compromising it in the eyes of other nations.

Even U.S. intelligence has fallen victim to cooptation by the White House to support military operations. The intelligence community, particularly the Central Intelligence Agency, has been compromised by the politicization of intelligence to support the use of force in Iraq and its cooptation by the Pentagon to support military operations rather than provide objective information. The Iraqi scandal, particularly the unverified claims that Iraq had a sufficient stock of weapons of mass destruction to constitute an imminent threat and that it was working closely with al Qaeda terrorists, has compromised not only the credibility of the intelligence community, but the nation as well.

A Fundamental Reorientation

Just over a decade ago, the West was celebrating the collapse of the Berlin Wall and the dissolution of the Soviet Union. The Cold War, we believed, had ended, creating a unique opportunity: The United States, as the surviving superpower, could undertake a new direction in foreign policy, leading the world toward a period of greater cooperation through the use of diplomacy, international organization, and international law.

This great opportunity is being squandered as the world drifts toward military anarchy, and even our own democracy is being compromised at home.

It is not impossible to counter this drift, but such a reversal would require a fundamental reorientation of the role of the United States in the world. A more hopeful and constructive foreign policy agenda would need to be based on a commitment to multilateralism and the rule of international law, on peacemaking not warmaking. It would need to promote global cooperation, rather than unilateral hegemony, as our main objective. . . .

The Bush doctrine and the neoconservative vision that undergirds it are recklessly endangering the international community and even our national security. Only a dramatically different vision can move us away from spiraling global violence and toward a more peaceful and just world, as well as a more secure and democratic society at home. This is the challenge we face today.

> *"'My way or no way' is no longer a tenable negotiating stance [for the United States]—even on military matters."*

The United States Should Improve Its Relationship with Europe

Jessica T. Matthews

Fundamental policy disagreements are causing a growing rift between the United States and Europe, argues Jessica T. Matthews in the following viewpoint. This divergence will be harmful to both the international community and the United States, she warns. In her opinion, America cannot continue to act solely on its own best interests; instead it must learn to cooperate with the nations of Europe. Matthews is president of the Carnegie Endowment for International Peace in Washington, D.C.

As you read, consider the following questions:

1. As explained by Matthews, how has an increase in the number of nonstate actors impacted the power that individual governments have on the international agenda?
2. How do the population and the gross domestic product of the European Union compare to those of the United States, as cited by the author?
3. According to Matthews, why will the United States be forced to carry a heavier diplomatic burden in the future?

In recent years, reaching back well before the present U.S. administration [that of George W. Bush], the United States and Europe have found themselves on opposite sides of a sobering—and rapidly growing—number of global issues. Taken together, these issues will determine the rules of the road for the future international system, and in doing so will have a lasting impact on the global distribution of wealth and the long-term security of individuals and nations. When the United States and Europe see eye to eye, there is little they cannot accomplish. When they do not agree, however, there is little they can achieve.

The Odd Man Out

Today's differences amount to much more than the quarrels among friends that have characterized the relationship for decades. Consider the recent record: In a solid bloc, the European Union (EU) approved, and the United States did not, the creation of the International Criminal Court (ICC), the Kyoto Protocol on climate change, the ban on antipersonnel land mines, the biodiversity treaty, and a verification mechanism for the Biological Weapons Control Treaty.[1] The two erstwhile allies are also deeply divided over a U.S. suggestion that it is prepared to abrogate the Anti-Ballistic Missile treaty unilaterally so that it might begin building an extensive national missile defense system.[2] Likewise, deep divisions exist over the Comprehensive Test Ban Treaty, a United Nations–brokered nonbinding treaty limiting exports of small arms, treatment of the environment in the World Trade Organization (WTO), and regulation of genetically modified (GM) foods. The two powers also have squabbled over support for the United Nations, the amount of resources that should be

1. The ICC was established in 2002 to prosecute individuals for genocide, war crimes, and crimes against humanity. The Kyoto Protocol aims to limit emissions of carbon dioxide and other greenhouse gases. Antipersonnel land mines often harm civilians long after a war has ended. The biodiversity treaty promotes the conservation of biological diversity and the sustainable use of biological resources. The Biological Weapons Control Treaty prohibits the development, production, and stockpiling of biological and toxic weapons; the United States withdrew from this treaty in 2001. 2. The Anti-Ballistic Missile treaty limits the antiballistic missile systems a country can use in defending areas against missile-delivered nuclear weapons. The United States signed this treaty with the Union of Soviet Socialist Republics in 1972, then withdrew in 2002.

invested in conflict prevention, and their respective contributions to international assistance.

Even taking into account that disputes get attention while cooperation passes largely unremarked, these differences illustrate a stark trend between long-standing allies that share deep political convictions and, presumably, the same long-term hopes for the world.

When U.S.-European disagreements touch upon traditional security issues, such as missile defense or biological-weapons verification, Europe still demurs. But the United States has time and again profoundly misjudged the world's new willingness to adopt international agreements—despite U.S. opposition—when those agreements have vigorous backing from the EU. As a result, Washington has repeatedly found itself on the wrong side of lopsided international judgments. The vote on the land mine ban was 142 to 0, with 18 abstentions; on the ICC it was 120 to 7, with 21 abstentions; and on Kyoto in 2001 it was 178 to 1, with only the United States opposed. The division on the nuclear test ban was similar.

With the exception of Israel and India, not a single democracy shared the U.S. view on any of these issues. Rather, the United States found itself in uncomfortable company with the likes of China, Cuba, Libya, Iraq, and Iran. While the individual merits of each of these decisions are open to debate, the pattern is unmistakably not in the U.S. interest. No country, no matter how strong, will remain a legitimate leader for long when it is the odd man out on so many decisions that command the support of the vast majority of the world's countries.

A Changing World

This strange situation has emerged from a decade of extraordinary upheaval. At its outset, the end of the Cold War meant the loss of the automatic deference accorded the United States as the leader in the fight against a common, mortal enemy. The absence of an external enemy, in turn, allowed domestic politics to acquire a much larger role in foreign policy on both sides of the Atlantic. And, in the United States, the end of that long conflict brought with it a much diminished willingness to spend effort and money on providing international public goods—everything from building new multilateral regimes and institutions to giving financial or technological aid.

In the midst of these dramatic changes, Europe has been engaged in nothing less than an attempt to invent a new kind of political unit—a historic development the United States has consistently underestimated. American experts prophesied failure every step along the way to the common currency. And they have let themselves be blinded by Europe's failures in the security realm to how much is being accomplished in the economic and political spheres.

Transatlantic Tension Unabated

U.S. Favorability Ratings

	Summer 2002 %	March 2003 %	May 2003 %	March 2004 %
Britain	75	48	70	58
France	63	31	43	37
Germany	61	25	45	38

The U.S. Is Overreacting to Terrorism

	April 2002 %	March 2004 %
Britain	30	57
Germany	33	49
France	20	33

Pew Research Center, March 16, 2004. www.people-press.org.

Since Europe's integration is a gigantic exercise in pooling, even perhaps in redefining, national sovereignty, it has particular consequences for the global agenda. For the sake of integration, Europeans have seen cherished national symbols changed, as happened with French cheese, Danish ham, and German beer, or eliminated as in the case of currencies. While plenty of doubts, discomforts, and even backlashes over the process have surfaced, it continues to roll forward.

The awkward mechanics of integration have allowed Europeans to acquire day-to-day experience—and hence a level of comfort—with exactly the kind of painful compromise, frustrating negotiations, and less-than-perfect outcomes that characterize multilateral problem solving in larger forums like the United Nations, the WTO, and the secretariats of major global treaties.

Globalization

Meanwhile, the integration of the European continent has been taking place against a backdrop of a broader form of integration in economics, politics, and information and communications technology. We call it globalization. One of globalization's principal effects is to shift activity into transnational space, whether it be geographic space (oceans and atmosphere), natural-resource space (climate, fisheries, and biodiversity), or cyberspace (monetary transactions and information). However, major international treaties and institutions do not recognize any type of transnational space. All of these institutions assume a 19th-century world in which everything of value lies neatly within some nation's borders. There is no political will to reinvent, or even to significantly amend, their charters. So as more political and economic activity shifts into this new transnational zone, we are stuck with a system of rules that ignores this emerging global landscape and has precious little institutional capacity to manage what happens in it. Globalization therefore means an ever larger and more demanding international agenda, more engagement by countries in each other's affairs over matters farther and farther behind each other's borders, and, even among friends, more collisions of interest.

Finally, this busy decade has seen a huge increase in the international role of nonstate actors, especially of multinational business and nongovernmental organizations (NGOs), but also of multinational bodies and criminal groups. This proliferation in the number of voices on the international stage democratizes but also greatly complicates international decision making. It puts greater weight on (and ensures greater difficulty in securing) domestic consensus before governments can even begin to negotiate. It means that governments have little control over what gets on the international agenda, much less the eventual outcome. The negotiations to ban antipersonnel land mines, for instance, began despite the united opposition of the five major powers (an obstacle that only a few years earlier would have guaranteed a diplomatic impasse). Taken together, these developments—globalization, the growing influence of nonstate actors, the emergence of the EU, and the decline of global U.S. leadership that came with the end of the Cold War—have rewritten the rules of international relations. The resulting cleavages among nations that remain close allies are not surprising.

The United States faces a relationship with the EU that is utterly different from either its relations with individual European countries or with U.S.-dominated NATO [North Atlantic Treaty Organization]. Economically, the EU is no longer a junior partner. It has a larger population than the United States, a larger percentage of world trade, and approximately equal gross domestic product (GDP). It pays a larger percentage of the U.N.'s core budget (37 percent versus the United States' 22 percent) and a much larger percentage of the U.N.'s funds and special program costs (50 percent versus the United States' 17 percent). On either a per capita or per-GDP basis, every one of its member countries contributes more to development assistance than does the United States.

For Washington, accustomed to receiving—or, if necessary, demanding—obeisance to its views from its European allies, this change has proved very hard to accommodate. . . .

Coming to Terms

For the United States, the first step in repairing its relationship with Europe is to recognize that NATO will no longer be what matters most. Relations will be determined more by the ever growing list of transnational issues that inevitably stem from globalization. America's European experts, who are NATOists rather than Europeanists, will have to be replaced with a generation that no longer sees Europe through that narrow lens.

At the same time, America will have to undergo the difficult psychological adjustment of recognizing that Europe is no longer the junior partner whose acquiescence to U.S. views can be taken for granted. That is already obvious in the economic realm, and as the years go by, Europe is likely to become more able and willing to accept heavier international political and security responsibilities as well. That will come, however, at an automatic cost in "followership": The United States cannot expect Europe to undertake heavier burdens solely at the United States' behest. . . .

How should the United States behave when disagreements do arise, as they inevitably will? Based on experience, it should drop its expectation that it can block agreements favored by a united Europe. When the great majority of the world's nations agree, the United States should expect to be among their number—not always, but more often than not. America's interests, not to mention its legitimacy and capability as a world leader, are better served by being a state party that can participate in shaping rules and procedures rather than in sulking outside the tent. Though Europe cannot challenge U.S. political or military supremacy, the world's single superpower must acknowledge that its power no longer translates, as it did during the Cold War, into a community of Western democracies and Third World dependents ready to fall into line behind U.S. leadership. Recognizing this reality will force the United States to carry a heavier diplomatic burden, but it will reduce the number of outcomes from which the United States is forced, in good judgment, to walk away. "My way or no way" is no longer a tenable negotiating stance—even on military matters.

An Immediate Priority

An immediate priority is to develop a constructive modus vivendi [manner of living] with existing regimes to which the United States does not now belong—notably the ICC and the Kyoto agreement—and to devise an effective verification mechanism for the biological-weapons control treaty. Addressing climate change is especially urgent: The longer the delay, the higher will be the eventual cost. And there is public and congressional support for finding a way back into a sensible international framework.

For its part, Europe needs to outgrow its knee-jerk criticism of the United States for either doing too much or too little, its too-often hypocritical international behavior, and its addiction to feel-good international agreements without regard to their content or actual ability to solve problems. . . .

The U.S. Mindset Must Change

Leaders on both sides of the Atlantic will have to adapt if they hope to close the widening gap that not only threatens the United States' ability to achieve its international aims but also greatly reduces the likelihood that global challenges can be met. Americans overwhelmingly support multilateral burden sharing and a U.S. leadership role considerably broader than its military one. At the same time, they have come to expect dominance. Congress especially has little patience for playing on international teams of which the United States is not the captain. It won't be easy to change this mindset, but the long-term costs of allowing the present trend to continue will exact a price Americans won't want to pay.

"It is . . . wrong to assume that policy change would eliminate hostile attitudes."

U.S. Actions Cannot Reduce European Anti-Americanism

Russell A. Berman

In the following viewpoint Russell A. Berman maintains that European anti-Americanism has intensified with the creation of the European Union. As the various nations in Europe have been forced to give up their unique identities in order to join the Union, they have searched for commonalities with their neighbors. Many now see anti-Americanism as a shared belief, one that binds the nations of Europe together. Since anti-Americanism has little to do with the reality of American life or policies, argues Berman, no matter what foreign policy decisions the United States makes, this prejudice will persist. Berman is a senior fellow at the Hoover Institution and Walter A. Haas Professor in the Humanities at Stanford University.

As you read, consider the following questions:
1. In the author's opinion, what has European opposition to U.S. actions in Afghanistan and Iraq revealed about the nature of anti-Americanism?
2. According to Berman, how is European anti-Americanism related to religion?
3. Why has anti-Americanism "provided an emotional underpinning" for many Europeans, as argued by the author?

Russell A. Berman, "America, Non!" *Hoover Digest*, Summer 2003, pp. 58–63. Copyright © 2003 by the Board of Trustees of the Leland Stanford Junior University. Reproduced by permission.

During the past year [2003] much attention has been paid to anti-Americanism in political life around the world. The argument is made that certain American policies provoke ill will and that, if it were not for these policies, the ugly face of anti-Americanism would dissolve into warm smiles of welcome. Not surprisingly; this proposition is typically put forward by domestic opponents of precisely those policies that, allegedly, elicit anti-Americanism overseas.

It is natural to wish that friendship replace hostility. It is also the case that anti-American protests do respond to particular policies: the rejection of the International Criminal Court,[1] the refusal of the Kyoto Treaty [to limit emissions of greenhouse gases], and, especially, the engagements in Afghanistan and Iraq. It is not always the case, however, that policies such as these are the root cause of anti-Americanism; it is therefore wrong to assume that policy change would eliminate hostile attitudes. On the contrary, anti-Americanism is a complex cultural phenomenon that reflects problematic issues in local cultures and deep features of global competition.

Distinct Regional Phenomena

To gauge the significance of anti-Americanism today, it is important to distinguish among distinct regional phenomena. Hostility toward the United States in parts of Latin America is a consequence of a long and troubled history, including the various interventions during the past century. Meanwhile, the American occupation presence in Japan sometimes leads to irritation around particular events. Obviously, these two examples are very different from each other, and neither is particularly related to current policy.

The Arab world offers a third example. In this case, anti-Americanism has been nurtured by the largely state-controlled press with its propagandistic treatment of the conflict between the Israelis and the Palestinians. Rather than underscoring anti-Americanism in the Arab world, however, it is more interesting to recognize its unexpectedly limited scope. Opponents of the wars in Afghanistan and

1. This court was established in 2002 to prosecute individuals for genocide, crimes against humanity, and war crimes. The United States initially signed the treaty but later withdrew its signature.

Iraq have regularly warned that provoking "the Arab street" would topple the moderate regimes in the region, conjuring up frightening images of unlimited fanaticism. So far, these worst-case predictions have not been fulfilled. Indeed, the large and most antagonistic demonstrations have not been in Cairo or Amman but in Europe.

European Anti-Americanism

The genuine epicenter of anti-Americanism today is in Europe, not in the Islamic world. Indeed it can be localized even further as "old Europe," the continental Western European countries, especially France and Germany but Spain and Italy as well. (In the latter two cases, the political leaders were willing to take a political risk and side with the United States, thereby resisting anti-American sentiment in their domestic publics.) In contrast, anti-Americanism is negligible in the "new Europe," the new democracies of Central and Eastern Europe. This difference within Europe became apparent in 2002: During President [George W.] Bush's visit to Berlin in May, he faced large, hostile demonstrations, but friendly crowds greeted him in November in Vilnius [Lithuania] and Bucharest [Romania]. One can easily explain a pro-American predisposition in the formerly communist countries, given the leadership role played by the United States in the Cold War. Explaining anti-American predispositions in the countries that have long been counted among our closest allies is a more difficult challenge.

Understanding this West European anti-Americanism is the crux of the matter. The accusation of anti-Americanism of course often elicits a defensive denial: The anti-American claims to be only "anti-Bush." Obviously it is important to distinguish between reasoned criticism of United States policy, as part of a vigorous public debate, and an anti-American animus that goes beyond reason, that takes on an irrational character, and that draws on underlying hostilities that have nothing to do with objective estimations of current affairs. It is a prejudice, and, as such, it is immune to rational objections.

One can observe three distinct aspects of the prejudicial character of the anti-American mentality in Western Europe. First, although anti-Americanism may point fingers at the United States, it is primarily an expression of local identity problems. German anti-Americanism always involves escaping a troubled national past, hence the constant Nazi metaphors. French anti-Americanism, in contrast, imagines retrieving a former great power status through a special relationship to the Arab world, hence the prominence of anti-Semitism and the violent attacks on Jewish demonstrators and Iraqi dissidents. Italian anti-Americanism, often moderated by the many transatlantic family ties, has largely been a vehicle to express opposition to [Italian prime minister Silvio] Berlusconi, unpopular on the Left long before his support for U.S. Iraq policy. In all three cases, it turns out that U.S. policy is really only a pretext for acting out local identity issues. Attacking an external scapegoat is a convenient camouflage for internal problems.

Hating America

Anti-Americanism now looms in the world's psyche without any of its erstwhile anchors. It isn't tempered by fear of a rival superpower; it isn't fortified by a vital economic or political alternative. And when American power is actually deployed, this free-floating animosity mutates into a kind of hatred. . . .

The anti-Americanism I'm speaking of is not designed to persuade the United States to alter its policies in one arena or another. It's designed to demonize the United States as a whole, to portray it as almost morally equivalent to the Islamist terrorism it is trying to hold back. This anti-Americanism . . . rarely proposes anything positive. And as it recites its mantras of anti-American contempt, and summons every American failing of the past 50 years without ever crediting America's successes, it marinates in its own resentment.

Andrew Sullivan, *American Enterprise*, April/May 2003.

Second, although anti-Americanism opposes U.S. foreign policy in the name of its presumed victims, there is no evidence of any particular solidarity with these countries prior to American engagement. The anti-American sector of the European public that has resisted, with increasing vehemence, the U.S. role in the Balkans, Afghanistan, and Iraq had previously expressed absolutely no interest in the misfortunes of the victims of Milosevic, the Taliban, or Saddam

Hussein.[2] Their suffering became noteworthy only at the point when the United States initiated attempts to bring such suffering to an end. There never were mass demonstrations in European capitals against any of these regimes; indeed opposition to regime change was the common denominator between the "European street" and the governments. Anti-Americanism is not concerned with the particular issues at hand but only in adopting an automatic opposition to any U.S. role. There is apparently no regime so wrong than an American effort to right it would not provoke protests.

Third, like any other prejudice, anti-Americanism is characterized by an ongoing loss of reality. It has little to do with the reality of American life or U.S. policies, and it is equally oblivious to the lives of the Afghans and Iraqis, who only serve as interchangeable tokens, pretexts for an obsessive hostility to the United States. Anti-Americanism offers a securely ideological worldview that will simply not yield to facts. Hence we see the grotesque willingness of large parts of the European mass media to treat the Iraqi information minister seriously, while directing unrelenting skepticism toward American reports. For anti-Americans, any evidence of American success can only have been fabricated, just as expressions of pro-American support on the part of Iraqis are denounced as counterfeit.

A Priori Hostility

Anti-Americanism functions like a prejudice in that it is impervious to facts. Debate and criticism of American policy are surely possible and legitimate, but an a priori hostility to American positions indicates a closed-minded ideology. It is important to consider the sources of this ideology.

Even today, European expectations regarding the United States depend on a distant history of the first encounters with the New World in the fifteenth and sixteenth centuries. From the European vantage point in the age of [explorer Christopher] Columbus, the Americas appeared to be realms of savagery and violence, extraordinary wealth, and threaten-

2. Slobodan Milosevic is the former president of Serbia, the Taliban formerly ruled Afghanistan, and Hussein is the former president of Iraq. All have been accused of human rights abuses.

ing power. These images formed a tradition, with both positive and negative versions: noble nature versus base violence. This tradition continues to structure the European perceptions of America and echoes through accusations of a "simplistic" foreign policy or the threat posed by a "hyperpower."

Religion also plays an important role in European attitudes. For American self-understanding, the search for religious freedom provides a foundation to national history. European anti-Americanism has inverted this story by accusing the United States of religious excess: too much moralizing, too emphatic a distinction between right and wrong, and too great a willingness to enter on "crusades." This religious anti-Americanism is not primarily about allegations of proximity between the current administration and the religious right. The criticism goes much deeper and locates a cultural deficiency rooted in that very first chapter of American history: the departure of Protestant sects from Europe in search of religious freedom. On a deep cultural level, European anti-Americanism resents that departure and views the United States in light of that original rejection. It even equates the United States with a Protestant fundamentalism that it places on a par with the Islamic fundamentalism of the terrorists.

The Ideology of the Hour

There is, however, a much more contemporary explanation for anti-Americanism in Europe. The current process of European unification is painful in many ways. The importance of long-standing national identities diminishes, as political authority shifts to the centralized European Union [E.U.] beyond significant local control. A so-called democracy deficit has resulted; most Europeans experience the E.U. as a primarily bureaucratic matter, lacking any compelling ideals or deep principles that could stir the hearts of the public. Anti-Americanism has filled that gap; it has become the European ideology of the hour, providing an emotional underpinning for a unified Europe that stands for nothing of its own, except its distance from Washington. The incapacity of the Europeans to act in concert, particularly in foreign policy matters, only adds fuel to the fire. Anti-Americanism is much less about the character of American actions than about the European inability to act at all.

Given the prejudicial character of European anti-Americanism, it is illusory to imagine that changing U.S. policy would significantly change European attitudes. European anti-Americanism will remain a fact of political life, at least until the Europeans come to grips with the standing of the E.U. and decide what sort of political role it might play in the world. In the meantime the clash of transatlantic civilizations is bound to continue.

Periodical Bibliography

The following articles have been selected to supplement the diverse views presented in this chapter.

Timothy Garton Ash — "Anti-Europeanism in America," *Hoover Digest*, Spring 2003.

Jeremy Bradshaw — "Europe Confronts Its Anti-Americanism," *NewsMax*, January 2004.

Stephen G. Brooks and William C. Wohlforth — "Global Predominance: American Primacy," *Current*, October 2002.

John Buell — "Security in an Age of Terrorism," *Progressive Populist*, May 15, 2004.

Wesley Clark — "Military Alliances: The Key to Victory," *Current*, January 2003.

Edward S. Herman — "Fog Watch: Nation-Busting Euphoria, Nation-Building Fatigue," *Z Magazine*, December 2002.

Michael Ignatieff — "The Burden," *New York Times Magazine*, January 5, 2003.

Sebastian Mallaby — "For a New 'Imperialism,'" *Washington Post National Weekly Edition*, May 17–23, 2004.

Joshua Micah Marshall — "Power Rangers," *New Yorker*, February 2, 2004.

Michael McFaul — "What Democracy Assistance Is . . . and Is Not," *Hoover Digest*, Winter 2005.

Jeffrey Record — "Nuclear Deterrence, Preventative War, and Counterproliferation," *Cato Policy Analysis*, July 8, 2004.

Robert J. Samuelson — "The Gulf of World Opinion," *Washington Post National Weekly Edition*, March 31–April 6, 2003.

Cal Thomas — "Towards a Moral Foreign Policy," *Conservative Chronicle*, December 1, 2004.

Helen Thomas — "The Way We Were," *Liberal Opinion Week*, September 2, 2002.

For Further Discussion

Chapter 1

1. List four pieces of evidence that Robert L. Bradley Jr. offers to support his argument that the United States will not run out of oil. In your opinion, which of these is the most convincing? Which is the least convincing? Explain.

2. Derrick Z. Jackson asserts that the environment is in crisis. Stephen Moore contends that pollution is actually becoming less severe. Based on your reading of these viewpoints, do you believe that America's lifestyle is causing an environmental crisis? Support your answer with examples from the viewpoints.

3. Four of the authors in Chapter 1 discuss America's dependence on oil as a source of energy. After reading the viewpoints by Emma Davy, Robert L. Bradley Jr., and Tom Solon, do you think that America faces an energy crisis in the future? What types of changes do you think America should make to avoid energy problems? Cite from the texts to back up your arguments.

Chapter 2

1. Linda Bren and Jeffrey M. Smith disagree on whether or not genetically engineered foods are beneficial and safe for human consumption. Based on your reading of these viewpoints, would you choose to eat genetically engineered foods? Explain, quoting from the texts to back up your answer.

2. Julian Gresser and James A. Cusumano maintain that hydrogen power will solve America's energy problems in the future. Michael Behar contends that America will not depend on hydrogen for its energy needs any time in the near future. After reading these viewpoints, do you think hydrogen is a viable energy source for the United States? Why or why not? Cite from the viewpoints to support your answer.

3. Lester R. Brown uses numerous statistics to back up his argument that the United States should expand its use of gas-electric automobiles. In your opinion, are these statistics convincing? Which is the strongest statistic presented? The weakest? Explain your choices.

Chapter 3

1. In Paul Krugman's opinion, a socialized health care system would solve many of America's health care problems. According to Jane Orient, however, socialized medicine would be harmful to the United States. Based on your reading of the viewpoints,

do you believe American health care should be socialized? Support your answer with specifics from the viewpoints.

2. Steven A. Camarota believes that high levels of immigration have a negative impact on the lives of Americans. Jacob G. Hornberger argues that this is incorrect. Which author presents the more persuasive evidence to back up his argument about the effect of immigrants on American society? Explain.

3. According to the Koret Task Force on K–12 Education, significant reforms are needed to improve America's educational system. List five pieces of evidence the task force uses to support its contention that the educational system is in crisis? In your opinion, is this evidence convincing? Why or why not?

4. George W. Bush and Douglas Holbrook disagree over whether or not private accounts should be created for social security. What points might these two authors agree on, however? Explain your answer.

Chapter 4

1. Spreading democracy overseas will make the United States safer, according to George W. Bush. On the other hand, Gerard Alexander argues that spreading democracy will not enhance U.S. security. Based on your reading of the viewpoints, which argument do you think is stronger? Why?

2. What arguments, examples, and statistics does Craig Eisendrath use to support his contention that the United States should not base its foreign policy on unilateralism and preemption? Which do you find most convincing? Which do you find least convincing? Why?

3. Jessica T. Matthews and Russell A. Berman discuss America's relationship with Europe. On what points do they agree? On what points do they differ? Which author's viewpoint more strongly influences your opinion on how the United States should react to European anti-Americanism? Why?

Organizations to Contact

American Enterprise Institute (AEI)
1150 Seventeenth St. NW, Washington, DC 20036
(202) 862-5800 • fax: (202) 862-7177
e-mail: info@aei.org • Web site: www.aei.org
The American Enterprise Institute for Public Policy is a scholarly research institute that is dedicated to preserving a strong foreign policy and national defense. AEI's publications include its magazine *American Enterprise* and books such as *An End to Evil: How to Win the War on Terror.* Articles, speeches, and seminar transcripts on American foreign relations are available on its Web site.

American Petroleum Institute (API)
1220 L St. NW, Washington, DC 20005
(202) 682-8000
Web site: www.api.org
The American Petroleum Institute is a trade association representing America's petroleum industry. Its activities include lobbying, conducting research, and setting technical standards for the petroleum industry. API publishes numerous position papers, reports, and information sheets.

Biotechnology Industry Organization (BIO)
1625 K St. NW, Suite 1100, Washington, DC 20006
(202) 857-0244 • fax: (202) 857-0237
e-mail: info@bio.org • Web site: www.bio.org
BIO is composed of companies engaged in industrial biotechnology. It monitors government actions that affect biotechnology and promotes increased public understanding of biotechnology through its educational activities and workshops. Its publications include the bimonthly newsletter *BIO Bulletin*, the periodical *BIO News*, and the book *Biotech for All.*

Brookings Institution
1775 Massachusetts Ave. NW, Washington, DC 20036
(202) 797-6000 • fax: (202) 797-6004
e-mail: brookinfo@brook.edu • Web site: www.brookings.org
The institution, founded in 1927, is a think tank that conducts research and education in foreign policy, health care, immigration, social security, energy, the environment, and other issues. Its publications include the quarterly *Brookings Review*, periodic *Policy Briefs*, and books such as *Protecting the American Homeland: One Year On.*

Cato Institute

1000 Massachusetts Ave. NW, Washington, DC 20001
(202) 842-0200 • fax: (202) 842-3490
e-mail: cato@cato.org • Web site: www.cato.org

The Cato Institute is a libertarian public policy research foundation dedicated to limiting the role of government and promoting individual liberty. The institute publishes the quarterly magazine *Regulation*, the bimonthly *Cato Policy Report*, and numerous papers dealing with issues facing America in the twenty-first century, including immigration, education, and health care.

Center for Immigration Studies (CIS)

1522 K St. NW, Suite 820, Washington, DC 20005
(202) 466-8185 • fax: (202) 466-8076
e-mail: center@cis.org • Web site: www.cis.org

CIS studies the effect of immigration on the economic, social, demographic, and environmental conditions in the United States. It believes that the large number of recent immigrants has become a burden on America and favors reforming immigration laws to make them consistent with U.S. interests. The center publishes reports, position papers, and the quarterly journal *Scope*.

Center for Studying Health System Change (HSC)

600 Maryland Ave. SW, #550, Washington, DC 20024
(202) 484-5261 • fax: (202) 484-9258
e-mail: hscinfo@hschange.org • Web site: www.hschange.org

The Center for Studying Health System Change is a nonpartisan policy research organization located in Washington, D.C. HSC designs and conducts studies focused on the U.S. health care system to inform the thinking and decisions of policy makers in government and private industry. The organization publishes issue briefs, community reports, tracking reports, data bulletins, and journal articles based on its research.

Competitive Enterprise Institute (CEI)

1001 Connecticut Ave. NW, Suite 1250, Washington, DC 20036
(202) 331-1010 • fax: (202) 331-0640
e-mail: info@cei.org • Web site: www.cei.org

CEI is a nonprofit public policy organization dedicated to the principles of free enterprise and limited government. The institute advocates removing government environmental regulations to establish a system in which the private sector is responsible for environment and energy policy. CEI's publications include the newsletter *Monthly Planet*, *On Point* policy briefs, and the books *Global Warming and Other Eco-Myths* and *The True State of the Planet*.

Council for Responsible Genetics
5 Upland Rd., Suite 3, Cambridge, MA 02140
(617) 868-0870 • fax: (617) 864-5164
e-mail: info@fbresearch.org • Web site: www.fbresearch.org

The council is a national organization of scientists, health professionals, trade unionists, women's health activists, and others who work to ensure that biotechnology is developed safely and in the public's interest. The council publishes the bimonthly newsletter *GeneWatch* and position papers on biotechology.

Environmental Protection Agency (EPA)
Ariel Ross Building
1200 Pennsylvania Ave. NW, Washington, DC 20460
(202) 272-0167
Web site: www.epa.gov

The EPA is the federal agency in charge of protecting the environment and controlling pollution. The agency works toward these goals by enacting and enforcing regulations, identifying and fining polluters, assisting local businesses and local environmental agencies, and cleaning up polluted sites. The EPA publishes periodic reports and the monthly *EPA Activities Update*.

Environment Canada
351 St. Joseph Blvd., Gratineau, QC K1A 0H3 Canada
(819) 997-2800 • fax: (819) 953-2225
e-mail: enviroinfo@ec.gc.ca • Web site: www.ec.gc.ca

Environment Canada is a department of the Canadian government. Its goal is the achievement of sustainable development in Canada through conservation and environmental protection. The department publishes reports, including "Environmental Signals 2003," and fact sheets on a number of topics, such as pollution prevention.

Heritage Foundation
214 Massachusetts Ave. NE, Washington, DC 20002
(202) 546-4400 • fax: (202) 546-8328
Web site: www.heritage.org

The Heritage Foundation is a public policy think tank that publishes research on numerous issues in twenty-first century America. Its publications include the quarterly journal *Policy Review*, brief *Executive Memorandum* editorials, and the longer *Backgrounder* studies.

Hoover Institution
Stanford University, Stanford, CA 94305
(650) 723-1754 • fax: (650) 723-1687
e-mail: horaney@hoover.stanford.edu
Web site: www-hoover.stanford.edu

The Hoover Institution is a public policy research center devoted to advanced study of issues, including health care, social security, immigration, and international affairs. It publishes the quarterly *Hoover Digest* and *Policy Review*, as well as a newsletter and special reports, including "Foreign Affairs for America in the Twenty-First Century."

International Association for Hydrogen Energy (IAHE)
PO Box 248266, Coral Gables, FL 33124
(305) 284-4666
Web site: www.iahe.org

The IAHE is a group of scientists and engineers professionally involved in the production and use of hydrogen. It sponsors international forums to further its goal of creating an energy system based on hydrogen. The IAHE publishes the monthly *International Journal for Hydrogen Energy*.

Natural Resources Defense Council (NRDC)
40 W. Twentieth St., New York, NY 10011
(212) 727-2700 • (212) 727-1773
e-mail: nrdcinfo@nrdc.org • Web site: www.nrdc.org

The NRDC is a nonprofit organization with more than four hundred thousand members. It uses laws and science to protect the environment, including wildlife and wild places. The NRDC publishes the quarterly magazine *OnEarth* and hundreds of reports, including "Development and Dollars," and the annual report, "Testing the Waters."

Property & Environment Research Center (PERC)
2048 Analysis Dr., Suite A, Bozeman, MT 59718
(406) 587-9591
e-mail: perc@perc.org • Web site: www.perc.org

PERC is a research and educational foundation that focuses primarily on environmental and natural-resource issues. Its approach emphasizes the use of the free market and the importance of private property rights in protecting the environment and finding new energy sources. Its publications include *PERC Viewpoint* and *PERC Reports*.

Renewable Fuels Association (RFA)
1 Massachusetts Ave. NW, Suite 820, Washington, DC 20001
(202) 289-3835 • fax: (202) 289-7519
e-mail: info@ethanolrfa.org • Web site: www.ethanolrfa.org

RFA comprises professionals who research, produce, and market renewable fuels, especially alcohol fuels. It also represents the renewable fuels industry before the federal government. RFA publishes the monthly newsletter *Ethanol Report*.

Sierra Club
85 Second St., 2nd Fl., San Francisco, CA 94105
(415) 977-5500
fax: (415) 977-5799
e-mail: information@sierraclub.org
Web site: www.sierraclub.org

The Sierra Club is a grassroots organization with chapters in every state that promotes the protection and conservation of natural resources. The organization maintains separate committees on air quality, global environment, and solid waste, among other environmental concerns, to help achieve its goals. It publishes books, fact sheets, the bimonthly magazine *Sierra*, and the *Planet* newsletter, which appears several times a year.

Urban Institute
2100 M St. NW, Washington, DC 20037
(202) 261-5244
e-mail: paffairs@ui.urban.org • Web site: www.urban.org

The Urban Institute investigates social and economic problems confronting the nation and analyzes efforts to solve these problems. In addition, it works to improve government decisions and their implementation and to increase citizen awareness about important public choices. It offers a wide variety of resources on education, health, and social security.

Bibliography of Books

Ronald M. Anderson, Thomas H. Rice, and Gerald F. Kominski, eds.
Changing the U.S. Health Care System: Key Issues in Health Services, Policy, and Management. San Francisco: Jossey-Bass, 2001.

Audrey R. Chapman and Mark S. Frankel, eds.
Designing Our Descendants: The Promises and Perils of Genetic Modification. Baltimore: Johns Hopkins University Press, 2003.

Lakshmanan Chidambaram and Ilze Igurs
Our Virtual World: The Transformation of Work, Play, and Life Via Technology. Hershey, PA: Idea Group, 2001.

Benjamin Compaine
The Digital Divide: Facing a Crisis or Creating a Myth? Cambridge, MA: MIT Press, 2001.

David M. Cutler
Your Money or Your Life: Strong Medicine for America's Health Care System. New York: Oxford University Press, 2004.

Roger Daniels and Otis L. Graham
Debating American Immigration, 1882–Present. Lanham, MD: Rowman & Littlefield, 2001.

Celia Deane-Drummond and Bronislaw Szerszynski
Reordering Nature: Theology, Society, and the New Genetics. London: T & T Clark, 2003.

Peter A. Diamond and Peter R. Orsag
Saving Social Security: A Balanced Approach. Washington, DC: Brookings Institution, 2004.

Simon Dresner
The Principles of Sustainability. London: Earthscan, 2002.

Richard Ellis
The Empty Ocean: Plundering the World's Marine Life. Washington, DC: Island Press/Shearwater Books, 2003.

Hilary French
Vanishing Borders: Protecting the Planet in the Age of Globalization. New York: W.W. Norton, 2000.

Simon Garfinkel
Database Nation: The Death of Privacy in the 21st Century. Cambridge, MA: O'Reilly & Associates, 2001.

Helene Hayes
U.S. Immigration Policy and the Undocumented: Ambivalent Laws, Furtive Lies. Westport, CT: Praeger, 2001.

Katrina vanden Heuvel, ed.
A Just Response: The Nation on Terrorism, Democracy, and September 11. New York: Thunder's Mouth, 2002.

Edward E. Hindson and Lee Frederickson
Future Wave: End Times, Prophecy, and the Technological Explosion. Eugene, OR: Harvest House, 2001.

Paul D. Houston   *Outlook and Perspective on American Education.* Lanham, MD: Scarecrow Education, 2004.

Philip Jacobs and John Rapoport   *The Economics of Health and Medical Care.* Sudbury, MA: Jones and Bartlett, 2004.

Gabriel Kolko   *Another Century of War?* New York: New Press, 2002.

Walter Laquer   *No End to War: Terrorism in the Twenty-First Century.* New York: Continuum, 2003.

James Larmine and Andrew Dick   *Fuel Cells Explained.* Etobicoke, ON: John Wiley and Sons, 2000.

Paul F. Lurquin   *High Tech Harvest: Understanding Genetically Modified Food Plants.* Boulder, CO: Westview, 2002.

Michael Mandelbaum   *The Ideas That Conquered the World: Peace, Democracy, and Free Markets in the Twenty-First Century.* New York: Public Affairs, 2002.

Robert C. Morris   *The Environmental Case for Nuclear Power: Economic, Medical, and Political.* St. Paul, MN: Paragon House, 2000.

Walter Mosley   *What Next: A Memoir Toward World Peace.* Baltimore: Black Classic, 2003.

Jim Motavalli   *Forward Drive: The Race to Build the Car of the Future.* San Francisco: Sierra Club, 2000.

Stephen Nottingham   *Eat Your Genes: How Genetically Modified Food Is Entering Our Diet.* New York: Zed, 2003.

Joseph S. Nye Jr.   *The Paradox of American Power: Why the World's Only Superpower Can't Go It Alone.* New York: Oxford University Press, 2002.

Richard C. Porter   *The Economics of Waste.* Washington, DC: Resources for the Future, 2002.

Kent E. Portney   *Taking Sustainability Seriously: Economic Development, the Environment, and Quality of Life in American Cities.* Cambridge, MA: MIT Press, 2003.

Marcus J. Ranum   *The Myth of Homeland Security.* Indianapolis: John Wiley and Sons, 2003.

Jean-François Revel   *Anti-Americanism.* Trans. Diarmid Cammell. San Francisco: Encounter, 2003.

Phillip C. Schlechty   *Creating Great Schools: Six Systems at the Heart of Educational Innovation.* San Francisco: Jossey-Bass, 2005.

William Shawcross   *Allies: The U.S., Britain, and Europe, and the War in Iraq.* New York: Public Affairs, 2004.

Vandana Shiva	*Water Wars: Privatization, Pollution, and Profit.* Cambridge, MA: South End Press, 2002.
Allen W. Smith	*The Looting of Social Security: How the Government Is Draining America's Retirement Account.* New York: Carroll & Graf, 2004.
Robert Sneddon	*Energy Alternatives.* Westport, CT: Heinemann Library, 2001.
Martin Teitel and Kimberly A. Wilson	*Genetically Engineered Food: Changing the Nature of Nature.* Rochester, VT: Park Street, 2001.
Craig Warkentin	*Reshaping World Politics.* Lanham, MD: Rowman & Littlefield, 2001.
Edward O. Wilson	*The Future of Life.* New York: Alfred A. Knopf, 2002.

Index

Adelman, M.A., 29
Affluent Society, The (Galbraith), 36
Afghanistan, 188, 202–203
African Americans, racial inequality and, 109–10
air pollution, 17, 18, 32, 36–38
Alexander, Gerard, 170
American Association of Retired Persons (AARP), 153
American Lung Association, 18
anti-Americanism
 in Europe, 203–207
 as regional phenomenon, 202–203
Anti-Ballistic Missile treaty, 194
anti-Semitism, 176
Arnold, Johann Christoph, 14
automobiles
 gas-electric hybrid, 87, 89
 hydrogen powered
  drawbacks to, 85–86
  U.S. research on, 83–84

Ballard, Geoffrey, 79, 85
Bargh, John A., 14–15
Becker, Dan, 44
Behar, Michael, 78
Berlusconi, Silvio, 204
Berman, Russell A., 201
Blair, Tony, 185
Bradley, Robert L., Jr., 25
Brandley, Mark, 28
Bren, Linda, 52
Brown, Lester R., 88
Bureau of Labor Statistics, 109
Bush, George H.W., 143
Bush, George W., 96–97, 116, 147, 163, 185
 education reforms of, 145
 environmental policies of, 33
 European protests against, 203
 hydrogen promoted by, 79, 83
 on nondemocratic regimes in Middle East, 172
 proposes expansion of nuclear power industry, 45, 47
 on spending priorities, 161

Bush administration, 187, 188
 has disregarded international law, 189–91

Caldicott, Helen, 46
Camarota, Steven A., 120
Census Bureau, U.S., 122
Center for Immigration Studies, 120
Central Intelligence Agency (CIA), 31, 191
Choudhury, Raj, 85
Churchill, Winston, 164–65, 169
Civil Rights Act (1964), 109
Clean Air Act (1970), 17
Clinton, Bill, 116, 180, 183
Coffman, Howard, 82
Cogan, John F., 118
Conko, Gregory, 50
Conzelmann, Guenter, 83
Council for Affordable Health Insurance, 119
Cresswell, Peter, 50
Crichton, Michael, 97
Cummins, Ronnie, 51
Current Science (magazine), 19
Cusumano, James A., 67

Davis, Patrick, 85
Davy, Emma, 19
democratization
 costs of, 175–76
 of Middle East, 166–68, 172–73
 risks of, 173–75
Department of Agriculture, U.S. (USDA), 55
developing nations, 32
Devlin, Peter, 84
Diamond, Larry, 167
Drexler, Eric, 95
Dunkley, Robert W.S., 96

Earth in the Balance (Gore), 36
Easterbrook, Gregg, 17
education
 has shown little improvement since 1970, 137–38
 higher-quality teachers are

needed in, 138–39, 146
impact of immigration on,
  122–23
reform of
  difficulty in, 139–40
  has been successful, 143–44
  principles in, 140–41
Ehrlich, Paul, 26, 37
Eisendrath, Craig, 184
employment, 112, 113
Environmental Protection Agency
  (EPA), 55
environmental stewardship, 31
European Union (EU), 196, 198
  anti-Americanism in, 199–200,
    203–205
  disagreements between U.S.
    and, 194–95

Federation for American
  Immigration Reform, 122
Fischlowitz, Bernie, 18
Food and Drug Administration
  (FDA), 62
  regulation of genetically
    modified products by, 55–57,
    60
foods, genetically modified (GM)
  allergies to, 63–64
  evidence of harm from, 62–63
  gene transfer and, 64–66
  regulation of, 55–60
foreign policy, U.S.
  economic aid as, 187–89
  multilateralist, 186–87
  unilateralist, 182–83, 187
Forest Service, U.S., 39
Freedom CAR program, 83, 87
Freeman, Robert, 70

Galbraith, John Kenneth, 36
gasoline, trend in price of, 91
genetic engineering, 50–51, 53, 54
  of foods, safety of, 55–57
Geneva Conventions, 189
globalization, 197–98
global warming, 2
GM foods. See foods, genetically
  modified
Gonsalves, Dennis, 53
Gore, Al, 36
Gresser, Julian, 67

Griffin, Michael D., 104

Hanson, Victor Davis, 178
health care/health insurance
  costs of, 112, 113, 122
  single-payer system of, is
    needed, 114
    con, 116–17
Helms, Jesse, 181, 187
Hett, Annabelle, 97
Hillesland, Marya, 32
Hindenburg disaster, 73
Hitler, Adolf, 180, 182
Hoffmann, Peter, 71
Holbrook, Douglas, 153
Holdren, John, 26
Hornberger, Jacob C., 128
Hubbard, R. Glenn, 118
Hubbert, M. King, 20, 26, 68
Hunt, James B., Jr., 142
Hussein, Saddam, 168, 177, 179
Hydrogen Economy: Opportunities,
  Costs, Barriers, and R&D Needs,
  The (National Research
  Council), 86
hydrogen fuel
  benefits of, 71–72
  as engine of economic growth,
    74–75
  global warming and production
    of, 82–83
  Iceland's success with, 84–85
  proposed program to promote,
    75–77
  safety of, 73
Hydrogen Highway Network
  Action Plan (California), 74, 84
Hype About Hydrogen, The
  (Romm), 87

immigrants
  assimilation of, 123–24
    multiculturalism and, 124–25
    obstacles to, 125–26
  consumption of public services
    by, 126, 131
  health care costs and, 122
immigration, 121, 122
  open, common objections to,
    132–34
  restrictions on
    are needed, 126–27

immoral results of, 130–32
Indian Council of Medical
  Research (ICMR), 62, 65
Intergovernmental Panel on
  Climate Change (IPCC), 28
International Court of Justice,
  189
International Criminal Court
  (ICC), 194
  U.S. rejection of, 190, 195, 202
International Monetary Fund, 189
Internet
  impact of, on social activities,
  14–15
  as news source, 13–14
  role of, in everyday life, 12–13
Iraq, 177, 187, 188
  anti-Americanism and, 202–203
  preemptive strike on, 180, 185

Jackson, Derrick Z., 30
Jacobs, Joanne, 13
Johnson, Lyndon, 119
Jordan, Barbara, 127

Kaiser Commission on Medicaid
  and the Uninsured, 113
Kass, Leon R., 51
Kean, Tom, 143
Kerry, John, 79
Kessler, Daniel P., 118
King, Colbert I., 139
Kirkpatrick, Jeane, 172, 175
Koret Task Force on K–12
  Education, 135
Krauthammer, Charles, 172
Krugman, Paul, 111, 116–19
Kyoto Protocol, 31, 194
  U.S. rejection of, 195, 202

land, suburban conversion of, 39
Leondar-Wright, Betsey, 110
Leone, Richard C., 162
Levy, Marc, 32–33
Lovins, Amory, 87

Malthus, Thomas, 40
Marchionni, Mary Jo, 14
Marshall Plan, 187
Maryanski, James, 54, 56
Matthews, Jessica T., 193
McClellan, Mark B., 54, 56–57

McKenna, Katelyn Y.A., 14–15
Medicaid, 112
Medicare, 112, 119
Middle East, anti-Americanism in,
  202–203
Miller, Henry I., 50
Milliken, JoAnn, 86
Mises, Ludwig von, 132
Monde, Le (newspaper), 185
Moore, Stephen, 34
Moore's Law, 95
multiculturalism, 124–25
multilateralism, 186–87

nanotechnology, 93
  potential of, 94–97, 98–99
  risks of, 97–98
National Academy of Sciences
  (NAS), 57, 62, 126
National Aeronautics and Space
  Administration (NASA), 100
National Commission on
  Excellence in Education, 136,
  137, 143
National Commission on
  Teaching and America's Future,
  146
National Endowment for
  Democracy, 166, 172
National Geographic (magazine), 26
National Hydrogen Association,
  72
National Research Council, 86
National Science Foundation, 94
National Urban League, 109
Nation at Risk, A (National
  Commission on Excellence in
  Education), 136, 137, 143
natural resources, 35
news, Internet as source of, 13–14
Nguyen, Ha, 161
No Child Left Behind, 145
Nuclear Energy Institute, 43
nuclear power, 43
  expense of, 45–46
  is safe alternative to fossil fuels,
  42
  con, 46–47

Ogden, Joan, 85
oil
  alternatives to, 23–24, 42, 70–77

conservation measures and
   independence from, 69–70
expansionist theory of, 26–27
imports of, 71, 91
remaining reserves of, 21
   are declining, 20, 22, 68–69
   con, 28–29
OPEC (Organization of
   Petroleum Exporting
   Countries), 22–23
opinion polls. *See* surveys
Organization for Economic
   Cooperation and Development
   (OECD), 57
Orient, Jane, 115
O'Rourke, Morgan, 93
O'Sullivan, John, 174

Pacific Research Institute, 36
Pershing, Jonathan, 87
Peterson, Christine, 95, 98
Pew Internet and American Life
   Project, 12
Pew Research Center, 196
polls. *See* surveys
pollution. *See* air pollution; water
   quality
Population Bomb, The (Ehrlich), 37
Porro, Bruno, 99
preemption, history of, 179–80
Prey (Crichton), 97–98

al Qaeda, 161, 162, 168, 188

racial inequality, 109–10
Raman, V.V., 12
Rauch, Jonathan, 17
Rheingold, Howard, 13
Rice, Condoleezza, 161
Roberts, Paul, 20, 22, 23
Romm, Joseph, 87
Roosevelt, Franklin D., 158
Rostenkowski, Dan, 116
Rumsfeld, Donald, 161, 191

Scheuer, Michael, 162
Schwartz, Joel, 17
Schwarzenegger, Arnold, 84
Seitles, Marc, 109
Sharansky, Natan, 176
Simon, Julian, 26
Smith, Jeffrey M., 61

Social Security, 148–49
   private accounts are needed to
      reform, 150–52
      con, 154–55
   reasonable reforms will
      strengthen, 155–57
Solon, Tom, 41
Soviet Union, Nazi invasion of,
   181–82
space
   exploration of
      guiding principles for, 101–103
      national benefits of, 104–106
      through robotics, 103–104
   militarization of, 190
Spencer, Jack, 161
Stalin, Joseph, 165
Stanford Institute for the
   Quantitative Study of Society, 14
State Department, U.S., 191
Sterling, Bruce, 13
Suez Crisis (1956), 182
Sullivan, Andrew, 204
surveys, 12, 35

Tanner, Michael, 131
technology, 125
   see also genetic engineering;
      nanotechnology
Tenet, George J., 161–62
Thucydides, 179
Tomorrow's Energy (Hoffmann), 71
"Twenty Hydrogen Myths"
   (Lovins), 87
Tyler, Tom R., 15

unilateralism, 182–83
United Nations, 194–95
United States, 31, 71, 189, 196
   defense spending by, 161, 191
   disagreements between EU and,
      194–95
   economy of, as obstacle to
      immigrant assimilation,
      125–26
   foreign-born population of, 121
   has history of support of
      democratization, 171–72
   needs to increase international
      cooperation, 199–200
   rejection of international law by,
      189–90

Social Security underscores
principles of, 157–58
see also foreign policy, U.S.

war on terrorism, 161–62, 165–66
was used to advance
neoconservative foreign policy,
185–86
water quality, 38–39
Williams, Arthur L., 18
wind energy, 92

hybrid cars and, 89–90
World Bank, 189
World Energy Council, 28
World Handbook (CIA), 31
World Trade Organization
(WTO), 194

Yucca Mountain nuclear waste
dump, 45

Zimmermann, Erich, 26, 27